The best of secrets should never be kept secret. Hurrah for Shannon's inspirational book, which takes enlightenment out of the "only for gurus" box to show us all how to experience and enjoy the profound transformation of a kundalini awakening. The instructional activities are practical and yet transcendent, ranging from meditation to cold water therapy, and even better, they acclimate the potent force of kundalini into our everyday lives. May you allow this book to leave the beauty mark of kundalini on your own body, mind, and soul.

—Cyndi Dale, author of *Energy Healing for*
Trauma, Stress & Chronic Illness

KUNDALINI
Energy

Shannon Yrizarry is a certified yoga teacher and professional clairvoyant who has written extensively in the wellness field. She teaches meditation and leads workshops on transforming the physical and emotional self through living a yogic lifestyle. She is also a certified Reiki practitioner and has done astrology readings, dream interpretations, and tarot for celebrities and television.

KUNDALINI
Energy

*Activate
Your Power
for
Enlightenment*

SHANNON YRIZARRY

Llewellyn Publications
WOODBURY, MINNESOTA

FIRST EDITION
First Printing, 2022

Cover design by Shannon McKuhen
Cover illustration by Rae Cook
Interior design by Rebecca Zins
Interior illustrations by Wen Hsu

Llewellyn Publications is a registered
trademark of Llewellyn Worldwide Ltd.

Library of Congress Cataloging-in-Publication Data
Names: Yrizarry, Shannon, author.
Title: Kundalini energy : activate your power for enlightenment / Shannon
   Yrizarry.
Description: First edition. | Woodbury, Minnesota : Llewellyn Publications,
   2022. | Includes bibliographical references and index. | Summary:
   "Kundalini can support your efforts to clear negative karma, strengthen
   your immune system, work through anxiety and depression, and improve
   your vitality. This book will teach you how to awaken your kundalini
   energy through yoga, breathwork, meditation, mantras, mudras, chakras,
   astrology, and more"—Provided by publisher.
Identifiers: LCCN 2021049107 (print) | LCCN 2021049108 (ebook) | ISBN
   9780738768281 | ISBN 9780738768397 (ebook)
Subjects: LCSH: Kundalini.
Classification: LCC BL1238.56.K86 Y75 2022 (print) | LCC BL1238.56.K86
   (ebook) | DDC 294.5/436—dc23/eng/20211117
LC record available at https://lccn.loc.gov/2021049107
LC ebook record available at https://lccn.loc.gov/2021049108

Llewellyn Publications
A Division of Llewellyn Worldwide Ltd.
2143 Wooddale Drive
Woodbury, MN 55125-2989
www.llewellyn.com

Printed in the United States of America

Contents

Contents

9: Cold Water Therapy   145

10: Following Astrology   151

11: Dreams and the Subconscious   165

Illustrations

Acknowledgments

I would like to express my deepest gratitude to Tej Kaur Khalsa and Harijiwan Khalsa, who have been anchors for my development as a teacher. Their exemplary selflessness and dedication to helping others offered me the inspiration to complete this book. I would like to thank Tina Fitzgerald, who gave me the opportunity to teach kundalini at her studio in Oceanside, California, which helped me see how a business can be run with conscious intention and thrive. I also would like to thank my dear friend Laura Hoff, who has supported me as a friend throughout the journey of writing, which has peaks and valleys as the creative process is both a walk in the dark and a path to the light.

Introduction

This book is designed to help you see beyond religion and dogma to distill the essence of enlightenment through the awakening of kundalini. With this book you will find out how to awaken your kundalini in order to experience pure contentment and no fear. You will know what you can do on a daily basis to find lasting happiness and see the ways it can bring benefits to your modern life.

As we see the common theme of kundalini throughout time and cultures, we see that spirituality can bring all cultures together in a common experience of peacefulness. At a time when the world is looking to rebuild after the pandemic, we need to understand how to work with our bodies to produce feelings of joy and a sense of calm so we no longer need to look to our material possessions, social status, or relationship status to feel that true satisfaction. When we strip ourselves down from our attachments and get the energy of the body harmonized through simple techniques, we connect to the universal consciousness that helps us know who we really are.

The approaches to experiencing enlightenment work with energy that has different names in different cultures. Kundalini energy is a common theme throughout the most advanced adepts in the exploration of human consciousness. But just how does this help us in our daily lives? It is the crux of empowerment in how we choose our partners, our food, our jobs, and our goals. As we begin the journey of awakening kundalini, know that this can transform your mind, body, and soul to find true happiness without having to subscribe to any system or spend money on the next best trending spiritual program. Kundalini reaches rich and poor alike, and it doesn't open faster based on your looks or income level. It is the ultimate equalizer as it helps us see that happiness is found beyond the hierarchies of modern life.

A Note About the Exercises

The kundalini yoga meditations, mantras, kriyas, and breathing exercises detailed in this book are mostly accessible through www.3ho.org for free. The resources in this book are only a small sampling of the thousands of exercises taught by Yogi Bhajan, who brought the kundalini yoga practice to the West in the early twentieth century. Keywords for searching YouTube are included to help you understand how to do the practices offered. Some links may change over time, so searching the name of the exercise can also provide ample video examples.

1

What Is Kundalini?

The experience of kundalini is that of heightened consciousness where one has increased creativity and perception of reality. It allows one to reach a state of oneness that could be called nirvana, heaven, or samadhi. In this state one feels connected to multiple states of consciousness where you can observe your ego and see how people think as a group. Beyond that, you can see the direction that can lead people to healing on an energetic level. It is quite literally a state of bliss where you feel totally at peace and feel like you understand life and your role in it. There are no deities that you must pay homage to in this state, but there are spirits in a nonphysical form you can be in touch with on an energetic and telepathic frequency.

One cannot discuss kundalini without mentioning the third eye, which is where intuitive visions arise. This is a part of our body that connects to our pineal gland in the brain. Much of learning how to access kundalini energy is centered around getting this gland to function. In order to understand what we are after, let's briefly explore how kundalini has been depicted in different cultures around the world.

The Greek symbol of the caduceus, with wings and two snakes wrapped around a rod, appeared in the medical field after the original symbol of a rod with one snake. The rod with a single snake represented the rod of Asclepius, god of medicine and healing. There are multiple scholarly theories about these symbols. The caduceus that became the symbol of the American Medical Association was the symbol of non-combatants for the US Army Medical Corps. The symbolism of a spiral energy around a rod indicates the relationship between kundalini energy and the spine. With modern life, our spine health is at an all-time low because of weak core muscles to hold it upright, lack of movement to keep it mobile, poor posture due to sitting and looking down, and toxins that affect the spine through the different systems in the body affected by toxic buildup.

The Physiology of Enlightenment

While both mystical literature and academia alike often seem to screw to the left ideologically, creating more distance between the student and concept of enlightenment by adding complexity, this technical perspective of enlightenment turns the screw to the right, bringing the one using the tool closer to the thing itself that the screw is hoping to secure. We are diving into the physiology of enlightenment seen through the similar practice that awakens kundalini energy cross-culturally. Physiology is the way in which a living organism or bodily part functions. This will help us understand what is happening in the body when we experience enlightenment, why there are so many common physical and mental methods across cultures of obtaining it, and why kundalini yoga provides a fast and direct map to technically expanding human consciousness.

Our modern age of electronic leashes, processed foods, fluoridated water, excessive sitting and sedentary lifestyles, and a work hard/play hard/party lifestyle all contribute to the deafening of our self-sensory system. From a more analytical perspective than it is usually presented in, enlightenment is a natural function of the body. When the body is not functioning optimally, our ability to sense to our full capacity is dulled. The good news is, the food habits and lifestyles of healthy people are also being spread through the wellness field, internet, social media influencers, and trends in the fitness industry. Meditation, yoga, and hybrid fitness programs are being brought to the masses to educate them on how to reclaim their ability to feel good and ultimately reach an expanded state of consciousness regularly. Instead of being reserved for those who can afford healthy food or the luxury of meditating copiously, enlightenment is becoming a common part of our daily goals and normalized more than ever in this modern age.

The biopiracy of our minds and bodies from toxic foods and toxic lifestyles has been a cultural trend that developed from the unbridled passion of the American dream, where instant gratification of get-rich-quick schemes were valued over the well-being of those buying the products. Luckily, cultural trends are shifting so people understand how their body responds to toxins and how they can unlock or "bio-hack" their energy. This information is spreading, with more large food brands taking an active role in promoting healthier products. The trend is not moving fast enough, though, and just as fast as people are working to help empower people to reclaim their energy, there are still companies pushing for the normalcy of toxic cultural programming because it is lucrative for many industries.

One way we can bypass the system is to understand the steps we can take to reach enlightenment in our own life. This book is going to help you understand very simple things you can do to reclaim the knowledge that will help you be the best version of you, where you feel happy, are intuitive, and know how to regulate your state of consciousness so that you can make more informed lifestyle choices. We may not think eating processed snacks from the vending machine is a big deal, but if it's part of the deadening of your senses so that you will struggle to have vitality, happiness, and enlightenment, well, that seemingly small decision is actually not casual but quite important and requires more careful scrutiny.

This concept of kundalini shows that the body is designed to give us the state of enlightenment, but we haven't turned on the switches. We need to get the eight main systems of the body functioning well so our energy can flow and we can increase our mental and energetic bandwidth. If this still feels like a far-out concept, don't feel discouraged. You will feel much clearer about it as you read this book. You will develop a better understanding of your nervous system, the glands in your body, the oxygen levels in your blood, and the energy that you can attain. You will see how you can use food, exercise, sleep, breathing, movement, and concentration exercises to amplify your intelligence, energy, and happiness. If you previously felt enlightenment was complex and elusive, prepare to find it simplified and accessible.

Kundalini in Different Cultures

EGYPTIAN HERMETICISM: The kundalini symbol is depicted as the staff of Hermes. Hermes is also known as Mercury, or the messenger planet. Hermes helped resurrect the dismembered Osirus, which is the life-giving or regenerative energy associated with the medical field today. Other symbols in Egyptian culture that represent kundalini reflect the mythology of creative energy in other cultures. Tet and Osiris represent the corresponding polarities with the female and male energy; the staff in Osiris's hand represents the spine. As in other cultures, the awakening of the brain and nervous system to reach superconsciousness is also depicted with Isis as a circular womb-like sphere where creative energy is activated. Even Isis has the lunar orb on her head, representing female energy; the ankh symbol in her hand represents the male energy, which together creates the flow of kundalini energy. Art also depicts the serpent emerging from the pharaoh's third eye.

INDIAN: The bliss that one experiences through the rising of energy along the spine through the energy centers is clearly laid out in artwork depicting Lord Shiva. Art from the Hindu culture depicts a serpent around Shiva's neck, and he also wears the moon on his head. An early Sumerian cultural seal depicts a meditator with an erect phallus, showing the reproductive energy being raised for spiritual progress. Icons within the long history of the many cultures of India depict the polarities and theme of bliss throughout them, including the dancing Shiva surrounded by flames of enlightenment. Tantric yoga trains adepts to convert sexual energy into spiritual power. Yogic practices depict a sleeping serpent that awakens and then activates the energy centers of the body.

CHINESE TAOISM: The symbol of the dancing yin and yang energies reflects the theme of balancing energy throughout the body. In esoteric Taoism, the feet remain rooted to the ground as one trains to experience the tao. Taoist yoga focuses on a methodical approach to bringing more energy into the system, which is geared toward creating a person who has controlled power that they understand and have mastery over. The ability to learn how to maneuver their own emotions and live in the world in a kind manner with this heightened awareness is a long process that has been taught for thousands of years. In this system, the student takes a long time to master their own energy and understand the state of oneness accessed through their yoga practices.

BUDDHIST: The state of nirvana is found through the devotion of purification of the mind, which reflects the Chinese Taoist yoga and Indian yogic philosophies of becoming a humble servant to humanity. The recitation of mantras, combined with meditation, is aimed at reaching a state of peace and ultimate compassion where one is not afraid of death and wants to help others. The expanded state of compassion is a result of the energy harmonized in the body, mind, and spirit, which is reached through raising the consciousness with sound and the activation of the third eye.

SOUTH AMERICAN: The third eye is depicted throughout the art of ancient South American cultures such as the Mayan, Inca, Aztec, Toltec, and others. Quetzalcoatl, which means "feathered serpent," represents death and resurrection and was the patron of the high priests. This deity represents life force energy and was said to be fire in the blood, which allows one to perceive both the physical and spiritual worlds and have control over the energy centers in the body.

~~~~~~

The idea that there is a creative energy that is somehow supercharged and can be brought into the body to expand consciousness and awaken the third eye is prevalent universally, and books could be written extensively on this theme throughout the world and its major religions and spiritual systems. But for the purposes of this book, we will present the concept in a way that is accessible to someone who works a job, has responsibilities, and needs something to help them feel good while living in the "real world."

We live in a technology-centric society and are constantly being affected by electromagnetic frequencies (EMFs). The teachings in this book will also help people strengthen their energy field to deal with the electromagnetic energy that is being amplified at a fast rate due to cell towers. This system is one that will help quickly boost the immune system to regenerate its function and the ability of the nervous system to respond and adapt to stress. The far-reaching applications of activating kundalini yoga are more relevant than ever, and this book is written to be readily adapted with easy practices that can be done at home.

Kundalini Will Help You in Daily Life

I want to convey as clearly as possible that what you will learn in this book has the potential to give your life an energetic overhaul. Energy is the basis of everything in our lives—from our interactions to our perceptions and our ability to experience joy. This book is not about promoting one system over another; rather, it will show you how so many spiritual systems are aiming toward the same peaceful state.

Kundalini is not just an idea to think about and hope that it is real. It is very real, and actually experiencing kundalini firsthand is what will bring these benefits to your life. Doing some of the things in this book is what will make the most difference. I'm not saying this book is the exhaustive resource for kundalini awakening either, but it is a great start and a succinct path.

This book is a starting point and a global perspective for your spiritual development. You can find more in-depth instructions for meditations and exercises on 3ho.org, which was the source for much of the ones in this book. Master kundalini teachers also offer streaming services with daily classes for very affordable rates. TejTV.yoga and Rama-TV.com offer classes online. You can also find classes for free on YouTube. In-person classes are becoming more readily available globally as well as at local yoga studios. Much of the kundalini yoga taught today and the practices in this book come through the lineage of Yogi Bhajan, a teacher who came from India and essentially spread this formerly secretive practice to the West.

When it comes to you in the real world, you stand to gain higher levels of energy, more self-confidence, greater health, stronger optimism, an increased creative instinct, the ability to connect with others peacefully, deeper relationships with others and yourself, the ability to attract more wealth, a greater awareness of your potential and the energy to live up to it. You will be able to face adversity with more strength, move through change without fear, and make choices that are truly going to be in your best interest instead of feeding your vices.

Kundalini doesn't make you want to run away from the world. It helps you feel joy from taking care of others and supporting the overall happiness of humankind. It's as if you suddenly feel a part of the sum total of the happiness in the world, and as you contribute to it by supporting others, you feel exponentially better as well. The spiritual teachers of many different lineages have had no problem giving up material possessions because they derived so much joy from helping others once their kundalini was awoken.

If the world can become more peaceful, happier, and kinder, every ounce of energy put into this book was worth it. At first you may not understand why to do the exercises because you haven't experienced the feeling of kundalini. Once you do, it will hook you like a delicious meal for your soul. Each time we reach that point of peace, we start to remember who we are and why we are here. Each time we feel a happiness that is self-generated, the world heals with us.

Experience the Supernatural

Kundalini awakening allows you to experience higher states of consciousness where you can sense things intuitively and know things by extracting them from universal consciousness. It's like plugging your mind into a huge document of information that you can use to maneuver through life. This may be precognition, intuition about what someone else is dealing with, or the ability to manifest and heal. Kundalini acts as a light to help you see through your third eye and step into the spiritual realms.

For those who live a lifestyle that is focused on kundalini awakening, they know that seeing the future is actually quite common for those who practice. Manifesting is something that happens when one becomes in tune with the cycles and laws of the universe. In the process of removing negative energy from the mind and consistently focusing it on elevated states of consciousness, you can bend time and space.

As you strengthen your own energy, you will have more to give. You will be able to help uplift people just by being around them, and you also will be able to direct healing energy and send it. Meeting with the souls of deceased teachers and saints is also common for those who have awakened kundalini.

The Process of Awakening

Kundalini awakening often happens gradually for people. They begin to crave being around kind people as their energetic sensitivity becomes more heightened. Sometimes there is a white flashing at the third eye as it opens that is there whether or not your eyes are actually open. As you start to increase the amount of energy in your system, you will often release old stuck emotional memories in the form of tears that seem to arise out of nowhere streaming down your face. This may happen years or days into the practice. Some people find that if they are really doing the work, they start processing a lot of their negative patterns to release them and will have both waves of more energy and the need to rest. When people have more energy of this kind, it's different than caffeinated energy in that it helps you order your thoughts and see what is most important to do with less effort.

One of the biggest side effects of the awakening process is feeling very positive. You may feel the "buzz" right away or it may take some time for the systems in your body to harmonize and feel the effects. If you have a lot of toxins in your body, you may experience detox symptoms that are temporarily flu-like but only while you're detoxing. You'll also probably notice a difference in your dreams. For some, they may have had lots of nightmares and then suddenly stop dreaming. Others may start to feel their dreams become very profound and otherworldly with messages for them.

Feeling energy release in your body is common with kundalini awakening. You may feel the energy as heat or like a tingling pressure. You may feel it shoot out of your arms, legs, or gather at your head. Sometimes your body temperature will increase and you may feel warm energy or hot energy at the base of your spine. In the unlikely event of spontaneous awakening, one may feel the energy shoot up the spine or it may feel like there is so much energy that it's hard to contain, which can make the hands shake. You may feel your senses become heightened so food tastes better and things look sharper and more vibrant.

People often get the feeling they have grown out of certain environments or groups as they awaken their kundalini. The desire to be around spiritual people becomes stronger, and you tend to crave more time to yourself to meditate than be around crowds. The need to sleep can be greatly reduced as the metabolism is also sped up. You may find your body rejects certain foods or is more sensitive to processed foods as the chemistry in your body changes in response to the practices and energetic shifts.

The Energetic Body

The aura is the energy around the body that interacts with the environment. This energy fluctuates depending on what is around you, planetary movements, geomagnetic energy, and the energy you generate with your thoughts. Being in nature helps to clear our energy field, as does breathwork, certain energy healing techniques like Reiki, and negative ions created by herb bundles, incense, moving water, plants, and some natural minerals such as sea salt, amethyst, and selenite.

The practice of kundalini yoga helps you expand your aura, remove negative lower vibrations from it, and charge it, which essentially makes you clear and intuitive. The kundalini yoga practice of wearing white is one way to slightly expand the aura because the frequency of the color interacts with the aura. Another way kundalini yogis have found to expand their energy field is by utilizing certain angles in movements where the energy enters the body much easier. Energy enters the body through energy centers and moves through the body. The energy field connects you to everything in a stream of information, including what people are thinking and feeling. Being able to intentionally pull in your energy field helps you not attract people who unconsciously are trying to get an energetic boost by being around you.

Taoist Dantian

Martial arts, which includes the practices of tai chi and qigong, teach about the energetic system of the body. The dantian are energy centers where students are taught to focus in order to activate more energy and direct the energy. This system shows three main energy centers that are rivers of qi, the life force energy. The bottom dantian is considered the most vital to activate one's intuition and power. Interestingly, the Hindu chakra system can be overlaid on this system, and the three yin chakras correspond to the dantian, with the four yin chakras in between them. The lowest dantian matches the location of the sacral chakra, where kundalini yogis combine prana and apana (*prana* is hot, yang, masculine, upward-moving energy and *apana* is cool, yin, feminine, downward-moving energy), then take the energy slightly lower to awaken kundalini energy.

The dantian are also a part of the most extensive map of the energy system, which is the meridian system used in traditional Chinese medicine (TCM). The practices of acupuncture and many Chinese medicine techniques are based on the body's energetic system. Learning this system takes extensive study and is beyond the scope of this book, but it is interesting to note that some very ancient kung fu moves only taught to advanced practitioners could paralyze or even kill someone just based on an in-depth understanding of the energy flow. The ancient kung fu masters, the Shaolin monks, are said to be able to do many of the same things that yogis with *siddhis* (powers) are said to do, such as levitate.

Hindu Chakras

The word *chakra* means "wheel" and refers to the seven centers of spiritual power in your body. According to the yogic system, each center is a bundle of nerves that energy flows through. The energetic body is very much like an electrical circuitry system in that it conducts energy, and the energy level can be increased, decreased, blocked, and opened. The chakras are a focal point for many of the movements, meditations, and breathing exercises in yoga. Traditional yoga was about building the

13

strength and flexibility to be able to sit in meditation and align these energy centers. Once they are on and active, the intuition is able to flow and one can tap into spiritual states of consciousness.

The chakras have alternating energies. The root chakra is yang, the sacral chakra is yin, the solar plexus is yang, the heart chakra is yin, the throat chakra is yang, the third eye chakra is yin, and the crown chakra is yang. A block in any of these or a weak energy flow will keep the kundalini from rising, so it becomes imperative to understand the nature of them to be able to see how your emotions and thoughts play a role in the awakening of your kundalini. Our thoughts and belief systems can create fears, anger, insecurities, timidness, jealousy, sadness, muddled thinking, and lack of true sense of purpose. All of these types of energies can block the flow of energy, and that is why kundalini yoga works to target emotional states more than just parts of the body.

The root chakra (base of the spine) controls energy levels. When blocked, you're fearful, unable to create stability, possibly have eating disorders, or hoard stuff because you are afraid to lose it. When it's flowing, you feel safe, you feel a sense of home, and you feel like you can provide for your basic needs. It links to the legs, feet, and colon.

The sacral chakra (just below the navel) controls your creative energy. When it's blocked, you may be afraid of intimacy or have an addiction. When it's flowing, you will feel creative and joyful, ready to use your energy to find ways to make things happen. It links to your hips, lower back, and reproductive organs.

The solar plexus chakra (upper stomach) controls your motivation. When it's not flowing, you will feel lazy, pessimistic, shy, or even be controlling and aggressive. When it's healthy and active, you are optimistic, laugh easily, will step into leadership, and have confidence. It's linked to the nerves, intestines, and diaphragm.

The heart chakra (chest) controls how we relate and develop relationships. If it's blocked, you will not be able to heal, you may have poor boundaries, and you may not love yourself. When it's flowing, you can process grief, start new relationships of all kinds, and grow. You are compelled to help people and take care of yourself. It is linked with your arms, heart, lungs, immune system, and upper back.

The throat chakra (neck) controls our speaking and how we express ourselves. If it's not flowing, we are either talking too much or unable to speak. We may lie or speak indirectly. When it's healthy and flowing, we can speak truthfully, effectively, and share openly. It's connected to the jaw, mouth, throat, thyroid, shoulders, and tongue.

The third eye chakra (brow) controls our mental function. If it's not active, we feel confused, we cannot create a vision for the future, and we have headaches as well as poor memory. When it's working well, we are intuitive, sharp, and feel like our thoughts help us instead of hinder us. This chakra is linked to the pineal gland, ears, nose, eyes, and parts of the brain.

The crown chakra (top of the head) controls our spiritual connection. If it's shut down, we feel depressed, isolated, and lack purpose. When it's flowing, we feel peace, expansion, and no fear of death. It's connected to parts of the brain, the hair, and the skin.

Our karma is stored in the arc lines outside of the body. This can be ancestral, coming from the family, or also from past lives. Men and women have an arc line like a halo from ear to ear, which is why spiritual art throughout the ages portrays a halo around the head. When the arc line is clear, a person has a sense of glowing because they are so pure. The actions in this lifetime can also affect the Akashic Records, where our words imprint like a computer dictation system. In the Akashic Records, we can access what our soul wants to do in this lifetime and what contracts we have to work through. This is why some people have a sense that they are meant to do something or that meeting someone feels more significant on a deep level.

~~~

Working on these energetic levels is common throughout many different spiritual paths. The soul is the energy that is outside of your body that stays with you for many lifetimes. It stores the energy of multiple lifetimes and the spirits of this lifetime you've created to help you achieve certain things. Working on a soul level with rebirthing techniques is part of the deeper energetic purification as you work toward enlightenment. Once all of your chakras are active and functioning, the perception of these more subtle energies is easier.

An Inspiring Story

Each chapter in this book includes personal experiences that I have had to help elucidate or display that there is validity to the concepts in the chapter. When I first was introduced to the concept of kundalini, I could not wrap my head around it. I wasn't sure I believed there was energy around the body, and I really didn't know if energy would raise up my spine and give me some eye-opening experience. Since I first started this journey exploring the concept of kundalini, I now have a vast array of experiences that are in many ways supernatural and profound. The stories I am sharing in this book may help ground some of the concepts for you and help you see how they may help you in real life.

I used to attend kundalini classes in Los Angeles, and the teachers would share stories that made the learning process more fun. When we had a glimpse into someone's real-life experience in relation to what we were working on, it was certainly inspiring. Author Doreen Virtue, who writes about spiritual topics, also includes personal stories in her books, which helped me tremendously when I was learning about these topics. So, for those of you who like stories and learn through them, I hope that these stories from my life enrich your own path toward what you are seeking.

The first encounter I had with kundalini yoga was in Newport Beach, California. I found myself in what seemed to be a very odd class. The teacher wore a brightly colored turban and walked into class carrying a large gong, a vat of tea, and a cushion. I was used to a teacher coming into class empty handed, so this was mildly entertaining, to say the least. I found that I couldn't really breathe deeply or for an extended period of time without feeling nauseous, out of breath, or irritated. I really did not understand the point of the class, which was about activating a chakra.

Over the next few months, I didn't make a conscious effort to go back to those classes, but somehow I started going more and more; there was something that kept me coming back. As an insecure twenty-something, I found it very fuddy-duddy. People didn't wear the sexy yoga clothes I was used to; they wore frumpy clothes that challenged my ego because I subconsciously still wanted to stand out in a group or at least feel like I was around sexy, cool people. I was still in a very toxic mindset. I had so much healing to do and didn't even know it.

My aversion to the class was there because it challenged all of my deepest fears. I didn't want to be considered "uncool," and I certainly didn't see the point of making myself feel nauseous in a class where the teacher had seemingly unrealistic physical expectations of my personal strength, stamina, and passion for a simple yoga class. It triggered me a lot. What I didn't realize is that it was putting me through a detox, and the nausea was because of that and not because the practice was flawed. I projected my issues onto the class and judged them, but luckily my judgments only kept me away for a few weeks at a time, and soon I found some peace in this teacher's Friday night meditation class, where we would stare at a dot or just be silent.

I was confused by the idea of "energy" and yet felt drawn to it. I found myself asking the teacher after class if he knew of an energy healing class where I could learn more. He said that he had one, and he gave me my first exercise to do at home. He smiled mysteriously and said something along the lines of "I don't know how it works, but it works." It was a kriya for abundance and quite complicated, with lots of things to do at once and five different parts.

I enrolled in his at-home mystery school, and it was around this time that I started to do my first daily kundalini practice. This kriya changed things in ways that seemed miraculous. At the time, I was a waitress and usually made about the same as the other waiters. But for some reason, while doing this kriya, I started making consistently more than the others and kept getting the best section in the restaurant. That was one of the first things I noticed during this forty-day journey.

Then I started to notice that what I would consider high-vibration people were consistently sitting in my section each day. Healers, celebrities, and mystical people kept being seated in my section, and the conversations and interactions I had on a daily basis became very inspiring. I distinctly remember one woman who felt she needed to meet me and was a dream interpreter; then there was a palm reader who told me very accurate things. The strange experiences did not stop there. I began to receive gifts and free things almost all the time. I remember walking into a coffee shop for the first time and they just said, "It's on us." I went to my usual haircutter and she refused to accept pay. I received a knock on my door and a neighbor I didn't know, who was a rep for a shoe company, was holding a bunch of brand-new shoes that happened to be in my size and exactly what I needed for work. The experiences were a direct result of charging my energy field and clearing negative energy, and I certainly felt more energetic and positive. I also had a high level of creativity and mapped out books I wanted to make. I made my first children's book and started to explore deeper in meditation easily. Needless to say, this Sobagh Kriya was life-changing. You can find it in chapter 4 and learn it for yourself.

I found that over the course of forty days, I became stronger and was able to extend the time I did the exercise up to the maximum allotted time of fifty-five minutes. That was when my energy was really expanded and my intuition became heightened. The more time I did the kundalini exercise, the more I was able to manifest and the more positive and loving my experiences were. It essentially alchemized my life. I was excited to share it with a coworker who had her PhD from Berkeley. After her first time doing it, she was excited to show me a gift she had received out of the blue from a student of hers.

Years later in Los Angeles, I shared this kriya with my personal circle of friends. One of them, a bass player in a band, decided to work with it daily. Soon he found himself touring the world, living in a place on the coast of Malibu, and making more money. After he did it daily for a year, he sent me $111 to say thank you for sharing it with him. To this day he has continued to expand. He now owns two homes in Nashville and has continued with his musical success, published a book, and had growth in relationships.

One student I taught this to reported that he was able to finally sell his property while doing the kriya, which helped him significantly lower his financial stress. He attributed it to the kriya and said he also randomly found money in his pocket.

One morning I woke up with extra energy and did the kriya for thirty-five minutes. It was a Monday, and I was supposed to do psychic readings at one of the company's locations that was always dead on Mondays. I did the meditation, went into work, and was stunned that my appointments were booked out. It was people who didn't know each other and all came in randomly that specific day. Each of them also tipped over 20 percent, which usually never happened. I can only attribute this to the kriya that I had done for a longer time than I usually did that very morning.

*Kundalini yoga is the science to unite
the finite with Infinity, and it's the art
to experience Infinity in the finite.*

Yogi Bhajan

2

Yoga and Kundalini

To help you understand the relationship between kundalini and yoga, we need to look at the origins of yoga. Yoga, which means "union," dates back thousands of years, and the original practices were called raj yoga or laya yoga. These teachings involved the study of the mind and body to expand consciousness and were not just about physical fitness and physical health, as some people consider yoga to be. Yoga was not originally just stretching but a series of esoteric lifestyle practices that opened one to the mysteries of the universe. These were not just ways to move the body; they were also practices for cleansing, fasting, meditating, breathing, mantras, and a study of human consciousness in relation to the planets and emotions. It's a very in-depth and complex system that now has many branches.

Kundalini yoga is very close to the original pure form of yoga. In West Hollywood many celebrities and artists swear by its transformative benefits. With the virtual world we live in, you can now study with the same teachers through online streaming at reasonable monthly prices, and they have free YouTube classes. The way that kundalini yoga is traced back to the more esoteric practices of yoga is from teacher to student. Today, students who studied with living masters are still teaching and tell stories of how, like an avatar, a master has certain abilities that seem superhuman, such as foretelling the future, controlling elements, mastering levitation, and having strong psychic vision. Once you start tapping into the higher states of consciousness, the physics that governs the higher laws of the universe becomes apparent and not merely a theoretical concept.

Just as any object becomes powered when the user knows how to operate it, yoga is a manual to help us operate our system. As a car is turned on with the turn of a key that unlocks its power, we also have certain locks that we can open with the keys of the very ancient yogic practices. During kundalini yoga you will benefit greatly from your practice if you first focus on the locks that help you move energy through the body by engaging certain muscles in conjunction with breathing techniques.

The Locks

You are going to learn some body movements or techniques that seem minor or strange but have a big effect on your energy. These small adjustments are going to make a big difference. When we first start learning a movement, we often think about the large gestures, but I encourage you to pay attention to the locks much more than you think you need to. In the poses and meditations, during the chanting and meditations, you will experience kundalini much quicker if you use the locks.

A part of the mechanism of awakening kundalini is using the locks so that the energy can activate the pineal gland and release your natural dimethyltryptamine (DMT), which is a naturally occurring psychedelic compound. If you've heard of the spirit molecule, it is dimethyltryptamine. This chemical is released through the process of kundalini rising. It allows the brain to be ultra creative and helps expand consciousness.

In order to access this, as well as allow energy to flow properly through the channels of the body, we need to know how to engage the lower, middle, and upper locks in the body to move energy. The chakras, which are energetic centers at nerve bundles in the body, will function better for the goal of awakening kundalini if you use the locks in meditation, breathwork, and chanting, as well as in yoga movements.

The lower lock is done by pulling the navel and sex organs up and in as if you're stopping the flow of urine. This is often compared to a kegel, which tightens the sex organs, and is also referred to as a root lock (*mula bandha* in Sanskrit). The second lock, done by pulling the navel up and in, is called navel lock (*uddiyana bandha*). The third lock is done by pulling your neck back in line with your spine and slightly tucking the chin as if to give yourself a double chin. This is called neck lock, or *jalandhara bandha*.

Creating a Daily Practice

One of the long-standing pillars of yoga is the emphasis on a daily practice. Consistent practice allows you to create momentum in your energetic reprogramming of the brain's neural pathways. In order to be able to perceive new realities and possibilities about the very nature of reality, doing so a little bit each day helps us get used to breaking through our limited or routine perspectives and start to experience the expanded states of consciousness. It also helps our muscles be able to hold us up longer and with less effort so we can go deeper into meditation. It additionally helps us build the muscles between the ribs that allow us to move the ribs wider and squeeze them tighter as we breathe. It conditions our breathing capacity so that we can take in more *prana* (life-force energy) and breathe more efficiently during our exercises. It helps us start to notice the mind and gain control over its tendencies to jump from one thing to the next without direction.

The flexibility one needs to have in order to allow kundalini energy to flow doesn't happen in one session of kundalini yoga. The suppleness of the joints happens as one detoxifies the body and starts to lubricate the joints. Similarly, the posture is corrected as the muscles lining the spine are rebuilt and the spine is held up so that kundalini energy can flow up the energy channels within the spinal column.

The subconscious mind, which is not discussed very much in many more modernized yoga classes that have a focus on fitness, is targeted in the practice of kundalini yoga in order to dismantle its power over your energy, your mind, and your ability to reach that experience of enlightenment. Because so many spiritual systems involve chanting, prayer, and movement, it's evident that there is a direct experience of peace as a result of these actions. Yogis who study these peaceful effects are able to explain the mechanics of how these actions affect the subconscious and provide the energetic relief we often experience regardless of which spiritual system we are practicing. When one chants a prayer or mantra, the directed energy moves the energy of the subconscious to help uplift a person's mood and release psychic pressure. As one works to create more positive neurological pathways in the subconscious mind, the ability to maintain a state of positivity and peacefulness becomes easier over time and with practice. The energy of the sound current is used in many religions and in non-religious spiritual systems because it creates self-hypnosis. Studies have found that it takes approximately twenty-one days to create a habit and for the mind to accept it as a regular part of your day. In the practice of kundalini yoga, one of the key facets of the practice is a stress on doing the same thing for a minimum of forty days because it works on the energy of the subconscious to create new neural patterns and then shifts your energy field instead of just practicing once and expecting a stupendous outcome.

"Tuning in" is what kundalini yogis refer to as reciting their opening intention-setting mantra. It is to set the intention to open to the higher spiritual helpers and teachers that have crossed over. It is to humble oneself and create a repetition in the mind that will help stop other thoughts that will distract from the meditation time. The mantra for self-hypnosis tune-in is *Ong namo guru dev namo*. It is repeated three times drawn out. The palms are rubbed together and then pressed together in front of the chest in prayer pose before you begin and while you chant. After

24

chanting, you take one deep breath, hold it for ten seconds, then exhale. It means "I bow to the great creative force and welcome the higher spiritual wisdom within."

You can also chant the protective mantra three times to protect your energy field from roving thoughtforms: *Ad guray nameh, jugad guray nameh, sat guray nameh, siri guru devay nameh.* It means "I bow to the primal wisdom, I bow to the wisdom through the ages, I bow to the true wisdom, I bow to the great unseen wisdom." Visualize energy going around you on all four sides as you chant. Then, when you're done with your practice, chant *Sat nam* once or three times to seal the energy and affirm that "Truth is my identity."

Strengthening Your Nervous System

With the world being introduced to a global pandemic for the first time since the Spanish influenza, people are talking about ways to boost the immune system. While kundalini yoga practices certainly do boost the body's line of defense in that system, it works on all the systems to bolster a higher voltage of the entire energy field to be able to withstand and fight off foreign pressures, toxins, and negative influences. That means your body will have less toxins, be able to withstand the pressure of stress easier, and be able to think more clearly because of pure oxygen in the blood that is not clouded with waste.

This mental acuity is perhaps the most valuable asset we can protect for the continued evolution toward a more peaceful and nonviolent global population. In both our personal life decisions and how we respond as a society, there are always actors who will try to elevate their own interests by taking advantage of those who are unable to think for themselves, whether it's a partner or friend taking advantage or an authoritarian government purposefully seeding spiritual exhaustion by capitalizing on fear and mistrust. The stronger your major systems are, the less likely you are to become sick or be easily controlled and the greater your capacity is to help those with weakened systems. I cannot think of a better way to help humanity than to strengthen your own nervous system through a yogic lifestyle, which leads to this universal experience of enlightenment.

Spiritual Teachers

The emphasis in kundalini yoga is to trust that your teacher—who hopefully has extensive experience in the higher realms, a strong practice, and deep intuition—will be able to help guide you in strengthening your intuition. A spiritual teacher can see things on an energetic level and understands the ways that psycho-magnetic thoughtforms block someone's progress on their path to enlightenment. In more simplistic terms, when someone is trying to better themselves, a spiritual teacher helps light the path for them to walk down and helps them see the other paths that are going to bring more pain and suffering. The teacher may be someone that speaks openly about the pressures of society to live up to certain standards. They may speak of the different ways in which toxins become a culturally normative and accepted part of our lifestyle, and they may speak to the behaviors in our lives that are blocking us from the universal experience of enlightenment, whether that means we are eating processed foods or allowing negative people to create fear-based thinking in us.

A spiritual teacher will have a wealth of information on the many facets of the yogic lifestyle and the daily practice, which for many people is an overhaul of habits in both what they do and how they think. In order to find the sources of toxicity in your life, it requires someone to help you see yourself; otherwise, you will stay in the fog of the ego and not the illumination of the higher planes of consciousness. While it is important to acknowledge the pain that people have experienced under the tutelage of teachers who missed the mark of perfection in many ways, it is also essential to highlight the development of those in many historic and present-day accounts who blossomed to be able to heal themselves and help others under the supervision of a spiritual teacher. Even teachers fall short of perfection, and we must remember they are human.

How does someone go about finding a spiritual teacher, and is it okay to study with different people or even online? This is where you can start using your own intuition. You may find that based on your work schedule, budget, or what feels right, there is an online subscription that is perfect for you at this juncture of your life. You may later feel called to travel to study with someone that seems to resonate with you. Perhaps you'll find someone in your local community that you can study with in person. The digital age is certainly allowing people to access the yogic tools at a faster rate than ever before, and you still need to use your own ability to check in with yourself about what is right for you.

Search for local teachers and try their classes or try some online classes and see how you feel with different teachers. You can also ask people who have been studying for a while what teachers they recommend or you can find local teachers by searching the International Kundalini Teachers Association (IKYTA) website at https://www.ikyta.org. Teachers with more experience have more to offer, and those who have published books or been teaching other teachers are certainly going to be able to offer you a deeper, more transformational breadth of wisdom.

Ultimately, the best teacher is yourself, and you never want to go against what feels right for you in your gut, regardless of what someone else tells you. The process of kundalini yoga is to awaken your inner teacher who holds the wisdom you need to reach the place of enlightenment. Your own work and humility will allow you to meet and develop a relationship with your own inner teacher.

The word *guru* is probably one of the most misunderstood words in the spiritual world. In Sanskrit the word means "teacher." But *gu* means "darkness," and *ru* means "light." The more esoteric meaning is moving from dark to light or bringing darkness to light, which, in a sense, could be understanding how to defeat the subconscious energy that keeps us trapped in an illusion of unhappiness. Maya, which is the illusion created by the ego, is a web of thoughts reinforced by the subconscious mind about the very nature of reality. Maya is the story of the collective consciousness that affects everyone on a subtle but powerful level. The other meanings of *guru* include "from the mouth of the teacher, master, guide, or expert." *Gu* also means "ignorance," and *ru* also means "dispeller." So *guru* can be understood as the person who removes darkness in the form of ignorance and someone who has great knowledge that they share.

While most people think of a guru as a physical person, it is actually something that is sought within yourself that is the true guru. This empowering truth is told by some teachers who have scrubbed their ego of the need for validation and aren't trying to get people to follow them. There is an ancient esoteric saying that when the student is ready, the teacher will appear. Having the intention to transform your life and grow may bring your teacher to you in the form of a challenging experience, a person teaching a class, a book, or a string of thoughts that allow you to see something differently. To the yogi, everything is one, so everything is the teacher. While that very statement seems to be hard to fathom, it is something that one experiences in a very real way when their vibration rises and they begin to see beyond the veil of the more basic laws of the universe to experience the multidimensional universe.

An Inspiring Story

As I began to study kundalini yoga more in depth, I heard stories of people having spontaneous awakenings. Teachers would sometimes give us instructions in class on what to do if someone experienced a sudden awakening. We were told to lay them on their back and massage their feet to help ground them. We were also told stories of people suddenly shooting up in the middle of a gong session (which is when the teacher plays the gong at the end of class) to an upright standing position or passing out from holding their breath too long, trying to get high after the teacher said to exhale. I never witnessed one of these extreme experiences in class and I still wasn't sure if this kundalini concept of energy rising was a real thing, even though I knew energy itself was definitely real. By this time I had been to psychics who had told me extremely accurate information, and I had a better understanding of how intuition worked. The serpent energy depicted in art and talked about still seemed like more of a concept than an actual part of my life—until I had a few more experiences.

I had lived in a house with people from around the world while doing my first yoga teacher training. One of the women and I got along because she was also watching YouTube videos about energy and going through an awakening. She told me that she had had an inexplicable kundalini rising while walking under a tree and that heat had shot up her spine and it was quite painful. She was not a student of kundalini yoga, but these stories of people suddenly having a release of energy are common in the spiritual community. She was always perplexed by the experience because she had no idea for a long time what had happened. When she told me the story, we both agreed that it sounded like a kundalini rising that happened spontaneously.

Another friend shared with me her kundalini experience after giving birth to twins: "I was on a hospital gurney and the nurses had just told me that they were discharging the babies but I had to stay in the ICU. Suddenly I felt this fire scorch up my spine, starting at the base, and I remember it caused my hips to arch off the bed like I was doing bridge pose. I yelped and asked the nurses if they'd just given me something or if the bed had an electrical charge, and they just looked at me like I was crazy! It wasn't until years later that I even learned what kundalini was and that I may have experienced a spontaneous kundalini rising."

Years later I would have frequent energy releases that felt completely different than anything I had experienced growing up. The first time it happened, I was in Orange County, California, at a kundalini studio. I was still a beginner and would attend the Friday night classes in Huntington Beach, where people always seemed extremely happy and friendly as if they were drinking, but all they had was yogi tea, which is essentially homemade chai. I remember being in a dark room and having my forehead on the ground in child's pose. I saw a flickering light and so I looked up, thinking a bulb must have been going out. But no light was flickering. I put my head back down and closed my eyes, but the flickering was still there. After class I asked the teacher what this was and she said it was my third eye opening, which was common in this class. I also experienced energy shooting out of my legs and feet in this studio while in downward facing dog pose. For a moment I thought something was wrong; it was like I was frozen, but electricity was pouring out of my feet. I had never felt anything like it. It was intense but not what I would describe as painful. It felt like a high voltage of energy was releasing for about a minute.

Years later I was doing more kundalini and had some similar experiences. One time I was at home and knew that I had been having energy shooting out of my feet pretty frequently. This time I made a mistake and forgot to move my laptop, which was placed at the bottom of my feet. As the energy began to shoot out of my feet, I suddenly realized my laptop was sitting there and rushed to move it, thinking the energy might mess it up. The next time I went to use it, it wouldn't turn on and was completely fried. I ended up having to get a new laptop. During my awakening phase years before, I had experienced electronics malfunctioning around me and one of my friends also going through an awakening. We would laugh as we would watch movies and they would freeze every time.

When I was practicing regularly, I would sometimes experience energy shooting out of my arms, but one time I was completely surprised when I was sitting in class and suddenly felt very warm energy at the base of my spine. I literally thought I had wet my pants and moved to check. It was the strangest sensation and lasted for about thirty seconds to a minute. This experience helped me realize that kundalini energy was indeed hot and at the base of the spine. I also experienced a fire-like feeling that didn't burn but was super intense in my stomach while in plow pose. It felt like the sun was in my stomach, with intense energy but not pain. It was just about the highest level of energy I felt I could handle and quite unlike anything I had ever experienced. Now I know it was my prana and apana mixing in the sacral chakra. Prana is the life force energy that helps move energy up the spine, while apana is the downward movement of energy that helps ground us. You can think of these as yin and yang as well.

3

Breathwork

W here one finds a system aiming toward the experience of enlightenment through the opening of the physical and energetic capac-
ities of the body, one finds breathwork. Tai chi, qigong, yoga, and clairvoyant training programs are all heavily dependent on the practice of
breathing deeply. The ability to control one's energy and strengthen it
is hugely dependent on the ability to consistently breathe deeply. Let's
say that the average person takes in 5 percent of their total breath capacity each minute. They aren't paying attention to their breath and they
receive little oxygen. The same person that breathes extremely deep for
one minute to the maximum capacity is increasing the energy in their
body and sending it throughout the body in the bloodstream to help
purify the blood and deliver it to the muscles, which need oxygen to
function.

From a technical standpoint, the mere action of deep breathing increases the function of the vital organs, the strength of the muscles, and much more. The physical sensation given to someone who breathes deeply even for a minute is one of instant positivity. The "oxygen high" is something that is working on many levels of the mind, body, and spirit. It also helps strengthen the body's energy field to help expel lower vibrations that hang out when our health is poor. The electromagnetic energy created by thoughtforms is cleansed by the breath, which brings life-force energy into our main energy channels and the energy field that surrounds us.

Breathing exercises are used to move energy and manifest because they can expand your energy field or be focused into a certain part of the body. It is widely accepted in the Eastern medicine world that the cells themselves hold memories and energy from the past. When we breathe deeply, we are able to release the lower vibrations stored in those cells to help energetically cleanse ourselves. There is also a physical detox that the oxygen helps with in the bloodstream. The practice of deep breathing strengthens the abdominal muscles, which are then able to massage the internal organs and help flush them. The abdominals are also better able to hold up the spine, giving the internal organs space. When the spine is upright, the prana that is brought in with breathing exercises is then able to spread and run through the energy centers instead of being stuck. Prana can become blocked at one location in the body, and breathwork helps add energy to help move that blockage.

A Common Cultural Practice

Breath has been seen as a route to transcending everyday consciousness and experiencing something supernatural that transcends our waking consciousness. From the African Kalahari Bushmen who used a shallow rapid breath to induce a connection to spiritual states of mind to the Japanese who used breathing techniques in martial arts to move the ki in their bodies, the breath has a long cross-cultural history of connecting humans with altered states of consciousness where they are able to perceive beyond the human ego. They tap into the universal consciousness or all-pervading energy to find answers. The Greeks, Chinese, Indians, Tibetan Vajrayanas, Buddhists, kundalini yogis, siddha yogis, Sufis, Taoists, and Essenes all have regarded the breath as the connection to the unseen power of life.

The Greeks had a word for "breath," *pneuma*, which also meant "spirit." The Latin word *spiritus* means "the intake of breath" and "spirit." In Chinese medicine, the word *chi* means both "breath" and "cosmic energy of life." The link between the act of breathing and the actual spirit/soul itself is seen through many cultures that included various methods of breathing to heal people, access wisdom, initiate pupils, and contact the spiritual realms. As we follow history and the development of new nations, we see cultures adopting breathing practices or recognizing the breath's spiritual power. These practices have been present in Africa, Asia, Europe, and modern Western culture. Psychologists have been studying the effects of breathwork on the emotions and the human psyche for decades. From traditional shamans to modern psychologists, there has been a ceremonial aspect to the process of breathing and reaching a more desired state of existence.

Pranayama

Now you will get the opportunity to learn some breathing techniques to increase your energy, help open your intuition, and raise your vibration through the harmonization of your body's systems. Pranayama is the branch within yoga that focuses on breathing. The word itself means to control the prana (life force) with certain techniques. If you ever saw movies where people were able to send energy out of their hands, well, this is one way to help make that possible.

As you do daily breathing exercises, your mind will start to be able to perceive things from a more intuitive perspective. You may find you get a headache at first from the increase in energy. You may find you feel a little shaky from the increase of energy as well. It's also not uncommon to feel slightly nauseous from it as it is helping detox your body. The energetic detox will continue to occur as you do the breathwork, and that often will release stuck emotions by making you cry. It's remarkable how many people find themselves suddenly bursting into tears in the middle of breathing exercises as an old energetic memory is released. Usually you'll know you're letting go of something because the memory will just pass through your mind as it is released. This is a great way to release old anger, fear, and resentment, and it can help you resolve issues in relationships especially with yourself. Breathwork helps you build confidence because it raises your vibration so you can perceive a more optimistic viewpoint. Breathing is said to create the "union" that is the very meaning of the word *yoga*. It is the connection to the energy of the cosmos, and it is the link to the experience of enlightenment.

There are a few precautions to mention about breathwork. Your body should not be forced to increase its electricity too quickly or it can create chest pain or, in a sense, blow out the nerves. You need to build up your breathing capacity over time and not just go from zero to sixty overnight. Navel pumping (pulling the navel in) is not advised if you've just eaten food or are pregnant or on your period. Start out doing less time in your breathing exercises and slowly work your way up to longer lengths in the exercises. If you've been doing breathing exercises sitting down, make sure to stand up carefully and slowly because it can make you lightheaded and dizzy. When you do breathwork, be sure to drink lots of water; before driving, have some food to ground you.

If you ever feel a sharp pain in your chest, sit cross-legged and put your hands on your knees. Breathe in powerfully through your nose and lift your shoulders up, squeezing your ears, and then drop your shoulders, just allowing gravity to bring them down as you exhale. Continue that rapidly for one minute and it is said that it can help prevent a heart attack. This could even be done in the car and could be a lifesaving technique when you truly need it.

Ujjayi: Victorious Breath
3–22 MINUTES

One thing corporate yoga has done pretty well is maintain a focus on slow deep breathing. This ensures that anyone, regardless of belief system, is going to start feeling the energetic benefits of the much wider world of yogic practices. The technique taught in most Western classes is called the ujjayi breath, which is slow and deep and only through the nose. It becomes more effective the more it is practiced because you get used to doing it and don't have to think about it as much. Also, over time, you're able to maintain the technique without stopping and your body will naturally start to use it to calm you down. The more you do it, the more your muscles are able to expand the rib cage to bring more prana into the body. The body is also detoxified through the exhale of air as it removes toxins through the breath.

To do this, sit in a cross-legged position with a straight spine. Constrict the back of your throat so that when you breathe in and out of your nose, it creates a sound like ocean waves crashing on the beach. This constricts the passageway so that less air passes through it, and it slows your breathing rate as well as allows you to take in more air. When you breathe in, first expand the lower lobes of the ribs and then the upper lobes, taking in as much air as possible, and then let the air out slowly. Maintain the constriction at the back of the throat and use this breathing technique to develop a calm state at any time. Begin with three minutes and then work up to five. Once you feel comfortable with five, increase to eleven, fifteen, and then twenty-two minutes.

You can choose to do this type of breathing all day if you want. The yogis have taught that in order to stay in a state of union all day, one can regulate the breathing continuously. Maintaining the ujjayi breath all day is something that can help you achieve a more enlightened state. It can be done quiet enough so no one notices and you don't weird people out or bother them!

Breath of Fire

3–31 MINUTES

This breathing technique can be used to help you recover from stress or burnout. Lots of people deal with low energy, and this can be caused by having a depleted nervous system. Many people are so exhausted that they don't have the energy to work out and just getting through the day is a challenge. For some, they are energetic but unable to think beyond the ego and still cannot find that state of bliss that many spiritual people talk about. The missing ingredient in many people's lives is having the right tools to activate the pineal gland, chakras, and aura to be in the frequency where they can sense our connectedness. One such tool is the breath of fire, which is a highly revered breathing technique in many yogic traditions. This technique can take some time to get down, but if you're persistent, you'll get it quickly.

The technique is done sitting in a cross-legged position with a straight spine or in a chair if sitting cross-legged isn't accessible. If you're in a chair, make sure your feet are flat on the floor and you're sitting up tall. Begin by forcefully pushing air out of your nose like you're trying to get a bug out that flew up it. When you quickly blow the air out, snap your belly in toward your spine at the same time. Let the inhale happen naturally through the nose and continue this process, emphasizing the exhale.

Start with three minutes. Work on creating a steady rhythm and a powerful breath that is continuous, as if it is one long breath. The more powerful you breathe, the more prana you will get. Once you feel as though you've mastered three minutes, move up to five minutes, then eleven minutes. You can go as long as twenty-two or thirty-one minutes. The numbers in the practice correspond to numerology. There is a reason that certain numbers are chosen, as numerology is the study of how numbers reveal a hidden order in the universal fabric of creation.

Alternate Nostril Breathing
3–5 MINUTES

This breathing technique will help you revitalize your energy. If you feel drained or don't feel positive, this can help you feel centered and restored. This works on both the yin and yang in your body and stimulates both brain hemispheres. You can use this to find a sense of balance and harmony. Start doing the breathing technique for just three minutes at first and work up to five minutes. Alternate nostril breathing will not just increase your energy, it will also instill a sense of calmness to help you be able to handle anxiety and negative emotions like anger.

Sit tall in a cross-legged position or in a chair. Use your right hand and block the right nostril with the thumb and alternate blocking the left nostril with your pointer finger. You'll start by blocking the left nostril and inhale through the right nostril. Close the right nostril and unblock the left nostril so you can breathe out of the left nostril. Breathe in the left nostril and then close the left nostril and breathe out of the right nostril. Breathe in the right nostril and continue this process for the remainder of your time. When you're finished, take a deep breath in, hold your breath for a few seconds, remove your hand, and exhale.

Lion's Breath (Simhasana)
3–5 MINUTES

This breath will help your physical body. We need the physical systems in the body functioning optimally for our energy to flow harmoniously. It helps your thyroid function and it helps detox your body. Energetically, it helps your throat chakra. The throat chakra will be covered more in the chapter on chakras, but know that your kundalini awakening will be thwarted if you do not speak directly and openly, which in today's society is not a common practice. Being overly polite because of fear of being judged or disliked is something that you can overcome with meditation and as you strengthen your energy field so you can overcome your insecurities. This breathing exercise brings oxygen and prana to this chakra to help clear the old stuck energy there from years or lifetimes of suppressed thoughts and emotions.

To do this breath, stick your tongue out so the tip touches your chin and breathe powerfully through your mouth without a raspy sound, which could hurt your vocal cords. Do this for three to five minutes. The breath is mostly concentrated in your upper chest and throat.

This breath is a powerful breath for stimulating the kundalini awakening. If you're going to practice it, take it up for a minimum of forty days to get the results.

Sitali Breath
3 MINUTES

This is a cooling breath that can help calm your mind when you're overstimulated, hot, or angry. This is another detoxifying breathing technique that will help rebuild your nervous system and expand your aura. All breathing techniques will help raise your frequency and allow your kundalini to rise if you have the proper spinal alignment, as we discussed with the locks.

Sit in a cross-legged position and stick your tongue out, curling it. Breathe in through your curled tongue and out through your nose. Fix your eyes at the tip of your nose. Make sure you're sitting up tall and you engage the root lock and neck lock. Continue this breathing process for three minutes daily and do it for a minimum of forty days. Your tongue may taste bitter at first during the detox and eventually turn sweet.

This will help heal your physical body by aiding the digestive system. The digestion is an essential system that must function well for harmony in the body so your kundalini can rise. Without regular daily elimination of toxins and waste, your body will be run down and lethargic, unable to reach the higher states of consciousness. A further discussion of the proper foods to eat to stimulate digestion will be discussed in subsequent chapters. Many of the poses and kriyas in this book will help your digestion as well. It has been said that digestion is the single most important component in your spiritual development.

Cannon Breath
3 MINUTES

This breath will help activate the relaxation response in your body, which is the function of the parasympathetic nervous system. All breathwork is detoxifying, and this particularly helps you shift your energy from negative to positive very quickly. The mouth is open with slightly pursed lips to create an O shape. The technique is basically the breath of fire technique but done through the mouth only. You focus on the exhale and snap your belly in on the exhale then allow the inhale to happen naturally. Be sure you're sitting up tall with the root lock and neck lock engaged. Continue for three minutes daily. If you want to experience the full benefits, practice it for a minimum of forty days.

Vatskar Breath
3–5 MINUTES

This is a sipping breath that helps calm and soothe the mind. Take eight little sips of air in through the mouth and then exhale through the nose. This will help you feel energized but calm. You can practice it for three to five minutes.

When we first start doing breathwork, it's common to pull the stomach in when inhaling but that blocks the expansion of the lungs. This is a good exercise to practice expanding the belly on the inhale and contracting the belly on the exhale. This will help condition your lungs to be able to do longer sets of breathwork such as thirty-one minutes of breath of fire.

Sitkari Breath

3–5 MINUTES

This is another cooling breath. It is done by keeping the teeth closed and breathing in through the teeth and then out through the nose. You can practice this if you feel impatient, angry, aggressive, or have a temper. We often think that we need to increase energy to raise kundalini, but it is better to think of it as having balanced energy. As you will see in the discussion of chakras, a chakra can be both underactive or overactive. If you have a need to control, you may want to practice this breathing technique to embrace a humbler, calmer energy in your mind.

Practice for three to five minutes. It will help slow your metabolic rate so that you do not have racing thoughts that cause anxiousness and impatience. Many people who "run hot" will benefit from this exercise and the sitali breath previously described. Someone with a lot of fire in their birth chart would also likely benefit from these two cooling exercises. The astrological components will be discussed in subsequent chapters.

An Inspiring Story

One New Year's Eve in Los Angeles, I decided to teach my friends a powerful kundalini breathing technique. We sat in a circle and covered our heads to prevent dizziness from the increased amount of prana we would get from thirty-one minutes of breathing. I told them that it was normal to cry when breathing for this amount of time so intensely. We chanted the protective mantra (see page 25) after tuning in and began a challenging kriya that I guided them through.

We wanted to bring in the new year in a way that was positive, healing, and would help us help others. We set the intention to clear negative blocks in our lives and held the intention as we breathed deeply together. Then, one by one, they started to cry. Almost every one of them had tears streaming down their face, and I was glad I had a box of tissues close. I had experienced the same release in this meditation myself and knew it was a powerful release of old stored energy. By the end of the meditation, there had been so much release that the women had makeup running down their neck. It was palpable how much we had accomplished as a group that New Year's Eve, and I was glad to have shared the technique with them.

All meditations and kriyas say they have a certain effect, and what can we do besides see if that is true? In kundalini yoga, every time I've earnestly picked up one of the breathing exercises, meditations, and kriyas, it has had the effects that it says it will have. I have also found that it usually offered more than what the written comments said it would offer.

When I was managing a kundalini studio, I used to sit down in front of my teacher for the noon class and uncontrollably burst into tears. His large energy field was so high vibration that it lifted things out of mine. I didn't know at this time what exactly was happening, but it felt significant and inexplicably powerful. Every day, like clockwork, I would sit—and boom, tears would stream down my face. I felt silly because I couldn't help it, but I knew it was helping me heal deep things. I took what this teacher said seriously and wrote down as much as I could. He isn't young and I know that each moment I can study with him is valuable. He once said that thirty-one minutes of breath of fire would be good to do daily, which I started doing. I didn't know what would happen, but what did happen was that every time I would do it, my thoughts would just automatically become more ordered and my creativity would just naturally turn on. I realized that when doing breathwork, I had to keep a pad of paper handy so that I could capture all the useful ideas that would suddenly hit me.

I also used the thirty-one minutes of breath of fire when I felt like life had given me just about all I could handle. I could tell that my body was struggling to handle the stress of a few very challenging life situations that all seemed to happen at the same time. I felt like I was raw, on the verge of a nervous breakdown, and I had no strength left. Every day for months I did the breathing, and it helped me recover from the stress that life had thrown at me. It helped me rebuild my nervous system and feel strong again, and it very truly saved my life.

4

Kriyas

*A*kriya is a set of actions designed to achieve a specific result. A kriya may involve breathwork, movement, chanting, meditation, poses, and mudras. Within a yoga discipline, it is a practice that is designed to achieve a goal in a defined area of life. While some kriyas are focused more on the physical body and its functions, all kriyas aid in the awakening of kundalini yoga. Do not get too stuck on trying to decide which kriya to work with; rather, make sure you do something and do it at least forty days in a row. The reason all kriyas work on raising kundalini energy is because they all help the overall picture, which is a complex interweaving of systems. We must not only work with the mind through meditation, just as we must not only work on the body through poses. Additionally, solely doing breathwork would not train the mind to achieve greater levels of awareness and subtlety on its own.

It has been said that hatha yoga, which mostly focuses on poses (*asanas*), is designed to prepare the body for meditation so that you may sit without distraction for long periods of time. Kriyas work on the trifecta of mind, body, and spirit to help you become a self-actualized human. The trifecta is a theme we see very frequently in many spiritual systems and religions. The Christian idea of the body of Christ, the heavenly father, and the holy spirit is one example. Could this be the symbolic mind, body, and spirit explained in a different way? The trinity concept wasn't new to the world when Christianity developed. It is deeply entrenched in Egyptian, Pagan, Persian, and Hindu cultures. The idea that three gods make one in Egypt combined Osiris, Horus, and Isis. In Hinduism they are Brahma, Vishnu, and Shiva. In Taoism there are three pure ones that are the three highest gods. In kundalini yoga there are three energies that run through the body to create a harmonic balance: ida, pingala, and sushmuna. The triquetra symbol predates Christianity in Swedish, Nordic, German, and Celtic inscriptions, and today it is widely used to represent the mind, body, and spirit.

The ida energy is cooling, feminine, negative energy linked to the moon and apana (in this case, negative doesn't mean bad; it's meant as the opposite flow of energy). This energy helps us eliminate waste and calms us. The pingala energy is positive and masculine energy linked to the sun and prana. This energy helps us create and stimulates the mind and the metabolism. The sushmuna channel is the center spinal channel around which these two energies spiral. In order to awaken the kundalini energy, the three must work together and move through the three locks. The process is one of thermodynamics (where energy cannot be destroyed), in which positive and negative energy (the energy of the sun and moon) are brought together.

Yogi Bhajan taught this process in a simple manner: the inhale brings in prana and the breath is held, pushing energy toward the navel chakra. The breath is let out and held out, which pulls apana energy from the root chakra to the navel. This creates a white heat, the sushmuna, at the navel. Then the focus and breathing techniques, including the locks, bring the energy to the root chakra, which stimulates the kundalini. Once the kundalini rises through the three locks and begins the stimulation of the pineal gland, it starts to activate the pituitary gland, which together creates what he called a "mystical marriage," opening the third eye so the crown chakra can open. When the pineal gland stimulates the pituitary, the pulses it emits back are all colors, which is why many people report seeing rainbow colors in their third eye as it opens.

In the ancient yogic tradition, the rajas, tamas, and sattva are the three energies, or conditions of matter, that permeate all creation. These are called the three gunas. Rajas is active/initiating, tamas is decay, and sattva is pure essence or saintliness. One kriya that helps bring these three into harmony is called tershula. It is a self-healing kriya that also allows one to send healing.

Before one performs kriyas in kundalini yoga, it is customary to first chant a mantra that raises the vibration and then chant one that protects the energy field. This is covered in chapter 5. As you will see, incantations are also a sacred ritual performed in many spiritual systems to aid the process of accessing divine/enlightened realms of consciousness.

You may notice that sometimes the terms *kriya* and *meditation* are used interchangeably. That is why there are some meditations listed in the kriyas chapter. There is a lot of overlap and not a fine distinction between them. It is most people's idea of meditation as "simply sitting" that makes it helpful to have separate chapters to present the information.

In kundalini yoga the exercises are not divided into levels. Therefore, it is up to the student to listen to their own body and modify as needed. Some people may choose to sit with their back against a wall for meditation or add extra cushion to their yoga mat by folding a blanket. If you are unable to do the exercise for the full length of time, just take a break and join back in when you can. If you don't have the flexibility to do a certain pose or have an injury that prevents it, focus on your breathing and do smaller movements. You have complete freedom to do this on your terms so that you do not feel pain and don't push yourself too hard. Sitting in a cross-legged position for extended periods of time may be difficult for a while, so if you need to uncross your legs or shorten the meditation, just do your best without causing yourself pain but still pushing to your personal edge. Even if you can only do a minute, it's better than nothing, and the next day you may find yourself able to do more.

Also please note that if there is an eye position mentioned, that is because the original text was written with that indication. If there is no mention of whether your eyes are open or focused at the brow or tip of the nose, etc., it's best to close them. Some meditations give you something to visualize, while others direct you to focus your mind on a specific area of the body. Not all were given with instructions for this aspect, but you can trust that you're going to get a benefit from the kriya whether or not you are given a specific focal point.

Manifesting

One of the more practical applications of awakened kundalini is the ability to direct energy for healing and manifesting. The creation process is something you will learn about more in later chapters about astrology and chakras. These kriyas are able to help you work on raising your vibration to awaken kundalini yoga and channel universal energy to manifest. This deeply esoteric knowledge is not to be taken lightly nor used to control or change anyone's free will, as it is widely known in the metaphysical community that doing so creates bad karma. That being said, we can also begin to understand the universal experience of miracles through the more refined study of the energy of the body in relation to the universe. Miraculous healings through prayer, hands-on healing, and manifestations are reported in numerous sacred texts. The *siddhis*—special powers we can awaken—are merely the more realized energetic potential of humans. Many cultures have reported those with special abilities, but the explanation was not often so readily available, nor was a way to re-create the power.

While many dark arts have a reputation for sorcery and ill will, kundalini yoga is not related to these traditions. Kundalini yoga is designed to help activate the upper energy channels of the body, which inspire one to live a more loving, pure, and saintly existence. The practices induce kindness, compassion, and love for humanity. To be ultra clear, this is not spellcasting; it allows one to amplify their thoughts and intentions. The practice of kundalini yoga amplifies your energy, making manifesting easier. This book strings a thread through time and space so you can see how helpful this practice is in reaching what so many people have written about and revered for all of human history.

Tershula Kriya
31 MINUTES

This kriya is best done later in the day when it is cool or in a cool room. It will generate heat in your body because it is going to stimulate the kundalini energy. It is one that requires focus and a longer-than-usual attention span for modern humans. The usual length of time it is practiced is thirty-one minutes. It is said to balance the three gunas and help kickstart the process of self-healing. It is also said to give you the power to heal someone by touching them or projecting your healing. It is one often used to cure fears and phobias, especially ones that have to do with a father figure.

The energy that is created is linked to Shiva, the destroyer or regenerator. Tershula is said to be the thunderbolt of Shiva. It has a remarkable effect and is able to help with psychological imbalances when practiced for a minimum of forty days in a row. Shiva is considered one of the

Hindu trinity of gods (Brahma, Vishnu, and Shiva). It will help balance all three nervous systems and improve mental disorders. It uses a mudra (a hand position) as well as the retention of the breath and a mental mantra that is only thought and not spoken.

PREPARATION: Sit with a straight, tall spine in a cross-legged position. You may want to sit on a cushion. Apply a light neck lock throughout the kriya. You will look at the back of your eyelids. Hold your elbows at the sides, touching the ribs, with your forearms out in front of you, bending your arms up so the forearms make about a 10-degree angle and the hands are slightly above the elbows. Have no bend in the wrists, with the fingers together and the thumbs to the sides. Place the right hand on the left, crossing at the fingertips but overlapped enough so that the fingertips extend past the crossing on each side. Make sure the palms are facing up.

BREATHING TECHNIQUE: Take a deep breath in your nose, pull back on your navel, and hold the breath as long as it is comfortable as you mentally recite the mantra and visualize your hands surrounded in white light. Exhale out of your nose and visualize lightning shooting out of your fingertips. Pull the root lock and hold the breath out as long as it is comfortably possible as you mentally recite the mantra. Continue this process.

MANTRA: (recite mentally) *Har Har Wha-hay Gu-roo*

TO FINISH: Relax the mudra and open your eyes.

You can view instructions for this meditation as well as hear the pronunciation with the world-renowned teacher Krishna Kaur if you search YouTube for "tershula kriya meditation Krishna Kaur."

Sudarshan Chakra Kriya
11–31 MINUTES

This kriya allows you to combine the power of visualization with mantra. It is said that it can help you rotate the psyche of the universe, which sounds pretty cool. Ultimately you are enhancing your visualization skills to create a very specific image while directing energy toward it to help it manifest. It will require your full concentration; start with eleven minutes and work up to thirty-one minutes. Instead of using head energy, this kriya will teach you to pray with your heart energy, which is more powerful and much faster. The heart is the largest chakra. For the best effect, do this for at least forty days in a row, focusing on what you want to manifest.

PREPARATION: Sit in a cross-legged position and keep your spine straight. Hold your thumb and pointer finger together in gyan mudra (see facing illustration), with your wrists resting on your knees. Your eyes will be closed.

MANTRA: Chant out loud and visualize energy leaving the back of your heart, circling up above your head, and then coming back into the front of your heart.

Aap Sahaae-e Hoaa: When you chant this, see the energy of the sound moving out of the back of your heart, going up.

Sachay Daa Sachaa Dhoaa: Visualize the energy going up to the ethers.

Har Har Har: Let the energy from the universe flow down and penetrate your heart, strengthening and purifying it. Pull in the navel slightly on each *Har*. When the energy comes down, you can visualize exactly what you want to manifest and see it filled with white light.

TO FINISH: Breathe in and hold the breath, mentally thinking "Pray and power," then "Realize the factual self of yours." Exhale and relax.

The statement at the end of the meditation was made by Yogi Bhajan and is meant to remind you of your true identity, which is a soul. We have kept the same wording to keep the teachings as pure as possible.

Please note that there is a popular sodarshan chakra kriya that is different than this, which is "sudarshan" with a U.

For this kriya, play a recording of the mantra *Aap Sahaa-ee Hoaa*. The recording by Nirinjan Kaur is excellent and easy to find; see YouTube.

Sobagh Kriya

3, 5, 7, OR 11 MINUTES EACH

The Sobagh kriya works by pulling energy into your aura and charging you with prana. It helps clear your aura so that your vibration is able to attract high-frequency people and things directly to you. This kriya is commonly used to attract money and opportunities. Each of the five exercises are to be done for the same length of time in one sitting of either three, five, seven, or eleven minutes each. It is said you should not go beyond eleven minutes for each of the exercises; if you do the full eleven minutes, the entire kriya takes fifty-five minutes. This kriya has two spellings, "sobagh" or "subagh."

> PREPARE FOR THE KRIYA: Sit in a cross-legged position with a straight spine. Using the Tantric *Har* mantra, which is easy to find online, can help you keep a steady rhythm in each exercise except the last one, which is done in complete silence. For the full effect of this meditation, do it for at least forty days in a row.

> PART ONE (NOT ILLUSTRATED): Your eyes will be looking at the tip of the nose. Hold your hands up as if you're reading a book, with fingers straight and in line with the wrists. Strike the sides of the index fingers together as the thumbs cross and the backs of your hands face you. Flip the palms and strike the sides of the hands and pinkies together. Continue alternating these positions as you say *Har* each time you strike and pull in the navel. The tongue hits the roof of the mouth on the "r," although it's pronounced *hud*. Continue for three minutes (or your chosen time), then inhale deeply, exhale, and relax for a few seconds.

> PART TWO: Reach your arms up to 60 degrees above your shoulders with your fingers spread wide (see facing illustration, top left). Eyes remain fixed at the tip of the nose. Breathe in through your nose intensely as you

mentally recite *Har* and cross your wrists (illustration, top right). Quickly spread your arms back to 60 degrees as you powerfully exhale out of your nose, again mentally reciting *Har*. Continue this in a steady rhythm but alternating which wrist is in front for the same length of time you did the first exercise. Inhale deeply, then exhale and relax for a few seconds.

PART THREE: Bring your arms back up to 60 degrees above your shoulders and make fists covering your thumbs (illustration, middle left). Make small circles with your arms (in, back, out, forward), using a forceful movement that shakes the spine as you complete the circles. Keep your eyes fixed at the tip of the nose and chant *God*, which is pronounced *gud*. Chant loudly, emphasizing the "d" as you pull in the navel in a steady rhythm for the same length of time as the first two exercises. Inhale deeply, then exhale and relax for a few seconds.

PART FOUR: Hold your hands like blades in front of the heart and slice them up and down, moving as high as the throat and as low as the navel as if you're rigorously cutting energetic cords (illustration, middle right). Move your arms rapidly as you recite *Har Haray Haree Wahe Guru* for one minute. Then whisper it as you continue to move your arms for a minute. Finally, whistle it, continuing the arm motion for one minute. Your eyes remain locked at the tip of the nose, nine-tenths closed throughout this, as with the first three exercises. Inhale deeply, then exhale and relax for a few seconds.

PART FIVE: This is done in total silence and stillness with your eyes closed. There is no mantra for this part. Hold your elbows up to the height of the shoulders with the right forearm resting on the left forearm (illustration, bottom center). Your arms create a box. Breathe in for twenty seconds, hold your breath in for twenty seconds, and breathe out for twenty seconds. Repeat this for the same length of time you did for the first exercises, then inhale deeply, exhale, and relax. It may be too difficult to do the full twenty-second cycle, so do a number that you are able to do; just make sure it's the same length of time for the inhale, hold, and exhale.

Sa Re Sa Sa
31 MINUTES

Also called Antar Naad mudra and Kabadshe meditation, this kriya is great to do before the next kriya (*Long Ek Ong Kars*) for a powerful manifesting combination. This will help open your chakras so that other mantras will be fully effective. This will make your words more powerful, and people will take you more seriously. You'll find you're able to manifest by speaking. Do it at least forty days in a row. It is recommended to do a minimum of ninety.

You'll be glad to know that chanting this for a minimum of forty days also brings prosperity and protection as well as creativity. Additionally, it is said to bring luck even to scoundrels.

PREPARATION: Sit in a cross-legged position with a straight spine and a light neck lock. Keep your arms straight, without a bend in the elbows, and press the tip of the thumb to the tip of the pinkie on both hands in Buddhi mudra. Extend the other three fingers and keep them together so there is one line of energy from the shoulder out through the tips of the three fingers. Listen to a recording of the mantra for a minute, feeling the mantra in your body, and then join.

MANTRA: *Saa Ray Saa Saa, Saa Ray Saa Saa,*
Saa Ray Saa Saa, Saa Rang, Har Ray Har Har,
Har Ray Har Har, Har Ray Har Har, Har Rang

TO FINISH: Relax the mudra and body.

～～～

This is an easy kriya to do for thirty-one minutes, but you may need to find a recording that you can chant with without straining your voice. The Nirinjan Kaur recording is a lower register for those who don't have a naturally high register. When you're chanting, make the tongue hit the roof of the mouth on all sounds except *Saa*. Pull in your navel slightly on each sound to create a pumping of your energy. Pull in the root lock slightly.

Long Ek Ong Kars
3, 11, or 31 minutes

Also called Long Chant, this kriya is known as the greatest divine key. It is not difficult, yet it is very powerful. It is said this can liberate you from the cycle of time and karma if chanted two and a half hours before the sun rises. It is extremely important that for the twenty-four hours after chanting this, you only think positively and focus on what you want to manifest because it will amplify your thoughts.

Practice this for a minimum of forty days for thirty-one minutes a day, and ideally use the *Sa Re Sa Sa* kriya before it. When the mantra is chanted with the neck lock, the prana and apana meet at the sushmuna and open the lock to connect you with the divine. It can be done any time of day. It will initiate your kundalini and balance your chakras.

You can start by practicing this for three minutes and then move up to eleven, and then to thirty-one.

PREPARATION: Sit in a cross-legged position with a strong neck lock. Place the thumb and pointer finger together in gyan mudra and rest your wrists on your knees.

BREATHING TECHNIQUE: You will breathe two and a half times for each round of chanting the mantra.

MANTRA: Breathe in and pull the navel in strongly as you quickly chant *Ek* while you focus on the root chakra. In the same breath, chant *Ong Kaar* in a drawn-out manner. On *Ong* focus on the sacral chakra, and on *Kaar* focus on the solar plexus chakra. Take a deep breath in the nose and pull in the navel as you say *Sat* quickly, focusing on the heart chakra, and then *Naam*, which is drawn out as you focus on the throat chakra. Right before you run out of air, quickly say *Siree* as you focus on the third eye brow point. Then take a half breath in and pull the navel in when you quickly chant *Whaa* and focus on the top of the head. Visualize the energy falling around you, back to the base of the spine, as you chant *Hay Guroo*. Try to keep the pitch from dropping.

TO FINISH: Relax the pose.

~~~~~~

It is best to use a recording of this and chant along with it until you get the hang of it. A great version to chant with and hear pronunciation is available if you search for "2½ hour long Ek Ong Kar meditation" on YouTube.

Healing

Addiction Meditation
3 MINUTES

Simply adding this three-minute meditation to your day can help you overcome behaviors that you feel you have no control over and will make you aware of addictions that are causing you distress such as food addictions or negative thinking addictions. If you're addicted to unhealthy relationships, addicted to feeling like a victim, or addicted to giving too much time and energy to people who don't deserve it, it can help with that as well.

This meditation works for recovery and addictions of many kinds. It can help you with addictions you aren't even aware of, such as thought patterns or neurotic behaviors. Do it at least three minutes each day for a minimum of forty days. It has been used for smoking, drinking, drugs, food, gambling, shopping, and many other types of addiction with great success.

> PREPARATION: You will sit in a cross-legged position and maintain a straight spine. Tuck your chin slightly to line up the back of the neck with the spine. For this meditation, your focus will be at the brow point with closed eyes. Bring your arms up with elbows to the sides. Make fists with the thumbs out. Press the thumbs gently on the temples. Keep the molars together and clench your jaw muscle four times as you breathe in for each syllable of the mantra and four times as you breathe out for each syllable of the mantra. You will feel the temples move each time you clench your jaw.

> BREATHING TECHNIQUE: Breathe in slowly through the nose, mentally reciting the mantra, and pull the navel in on each syllable. Breathe out slowly through the nose, mentally reciting the mantra, and pull the navel in on each syllable.

MANTRA: *Sa Ta Na Ma* (recited mentally)

TO FINISH: Relax the pose.

～～～

You can find many videos of this meditation if you search for "kundalini yoga addiction meditation" on YouTube.

Meditation to Heal a Broken Heart
22 MINUTES

When we go through a breakup, heartache is a real physical experience. The emotions damage the nerves just as a wound damages the flesh. In order to repair the nerves, energy must be rebuilt. This meditation is to repair the nerves in the heart chakra to heal from heartbreak. After forty days you'll feel significantly different.

PREPARATION: Sit in a cross-legged position with a straight spine. Tuck your chin slightly to line up the back of the neck with the spine. Bring your elbows out to the sides and press your palms together. Line up the top of the middle fingers with your brow point, which is the third eye. Eyes are to remain closed. Continue for twenty minutes.

BREATHING TECHNIQUE: Breathing is normal through the nose.

MANTRA: no mantra specified.

TO FINISH: Inhale and then exhale. Breathe normally again through the nose as you interlace hands and stretch your arms above your head for two minutes.

～～～

You can find a video of this meditation if you search for "heart healing meridian meditation for a broken heart Brett Larkin" on YouTube.

Ra Ma Da Sa

11–31 MINUTES

Also called Siri Gaitri Mantra, this kriya allows you to capture the healing energy of the universe. You can also use it to heal others. It can be done from eleven to thirty-one minutes. This will change the frequency of your body as it stimulates the kundalini energy directly. Practice this for at least forty days.

> PREPARATION: Sit in a cross-legged position with a straight spine and a light neck lock.
>
> MANTRA: *Raa Maa Daa Saa, Saa Say So Hang*
>
> TO FINISH: Inhale powerfully and hold your breath, visualizing whomever you want to heal as healed and strong and surrounded by white light. Exhale and then do it one more time. Raise your arms and shake your hands.

~~~~~~~~~~

There is a specific melody to this kriya, so find a recording of it to chant along with: search "Ra Ma Da Sa Snatam Kaur" on YouTube. There are eight syllables, and you can pull your navel in slightly on each, but really pull it in on the fourth and eighth (*Saa* and *Hang*). The first part brings your energy up to the ethers; the second part brings the ethers down to you. You can also find a video of this meditation if you search for "Ra Ma Da Sa healing meditation Kimilla."

Clearing Karma

Meditation to Remove Ancestral Karma
31 MINUTES

The energy we inherit from our family can lead to addiction. One way to counteract the energy we've inherited is to confront it and dislodge it with our intention and the power of sound and breath. This meditation helps clear you from the karmic patterns you've inherited and will help you best if done a minimum of forty days. This clears the negative energy in your aura as well and will make you feel light. You may cry from the release as you dislodge old emotional energy. This helps you see beyond duality to true reality. When you do not see reality, there is humongous pain. This will help you experience that infinity is within you, not outside of you.

PREPARATION: Sit in a cross-legged position with a straight spine. Tuck your chin slightly so the back of the neck is in line with the spine. Pull the navel in on each *Wahe Guru* or *Wahe Jio* during the meditation. Eyes will be closed for this meditation. Your hands are in front of you, with elbows bent as if you're cupping water (see illustration, left). You scoop up and over your head and flick the wrists behind you as if throwing away old energy (illustration, right). Every time the song says *Wahe Guru* or *Wahe Jio,* you will make one full scoop, ending with your hands back at the beginning position. It's about one scoop per second.

BREATHING TECHNIQUE: Powerfully inhale through the nose as you scoop your arms up and over and then exhale through the nose as you bring them back to the original position.

MANTRA: *Wahe Guru, Wahe Guru, Wahe Guru, Wahe Jio*

TO FINISH: Inhale and lift your arms up and reach back as you hold your breath for fifteen seconds. Exhale and relax. Inhale and reach back again for fifteen seconds. Exhale and relax. Repeat once more.

～～～

Available on *Morning Sadhana Album* by Gyani Ji. This is the version that should be played. Listen to the mantra and recite it mentally. You can view a video of this meditation if you search "meditation to clear karma by Nicole Nardone" on YouTube.

Anxiety/Depression

Now, more than any other time in human history, our nervous system is overwhelmed with stimulation. With our electronic leashes and constant alerts, our attention is pulled in different directions, lowering our ability to relax throughout the day. With the onset of technology connecting us globally, we are able to access opportunities, relationships, and people around the world in infinite supply. The amount of decisions we are making, as well as the amount of information we are processing, is overwhelming on a subtle level. In order to "keep up," we need to add energy to our nervous system in order to think clearly and still remain in control of our minds. Each of these meditations involves breathing techniques that will help you regulate your nerves and emotions and give you the ability to cope with the changing times.

Meditation for Emotional Balance
3 MINUTES

This is one of those meditations you want to have in your emotional tool kit. It is perfect to use when you are upset. If someone did something that has made you very emotional or something has happened and you need to calm down, do this meditation. By regulating your breath and hydrating, you will start to feel better. It makes you feel safe and pulls you out of the state you are in very quickly. The reason drinking water is a part of the meditation is that dehydration causes emotional upset because of pressure on the kidneys. This meditation helps your brain by regulating the element of water and air. This is a great meditation to do quickly when you're unsure what to do and when you feel like you're going to explode with emotion.

> PREPARATION: Drink a glass of water before you begin. Sit in a cross-legged position and tuck your chin to line up the back of the neck with the spine. Sit up straight. The meditation is done with the eyes closed. Cross your arms and tuck your hands into your armpits. Scrunch your shoulders up by your ears and keep them there.

> BREATHING TECHNIQUE: Your breath will naturally become slow as you breathe through your nose in this position for three minutes.

> TO FINISH: Relax the pose.

You can view a video of this meditation if you search "meditation for emotional balance kundalini yoga for women" on YouTube.

Beyond Stress and Duality
11 MINUTES

This is a great meditation to combat stress because it helps strengthen your nerves and balance the brain. Meridians on the ends of your fingers correspond to points in the brain to bring balance between the two brain hemispheres. If you struggle to make decisions, this will help you decide. After doing this meditation, you'll feel you can respond to stressful situations easier, and it can help you cope after trauma. The breathing helps you remain calm throughout the day and will give you mental clarity. A lot of stress today comes from inner conflicts about how to proceed in life in small and big ways. You can work to overcome that with this technique, which builds intuition on the best course for your own highest good.

PREPARATION: Sit in a cross-legged position so that your spine is straight. Tuck your chin slightly so the back of the neck lines up with the spine. Bring your elbows to the sides so your fingertips meet, but keep the palms apart. Point your thumbs toward you and put enough pressure on the fingers that the first segment of the fingers touches on opposite hands and the fingers spread. Your eye focus will be at the tip of the nose.

BREATHING TECHNIQUE: Breathe in deeply and slowly through your nose and then out through pursed lips for eight strokes in a steady rhythm. This means divide the exhale into eight equal little exhales. Pull your navel in on each stroke. Continue for eleven minutes.

TO FINISH: Take a deep inhale and hold your breath for ten to thirty seconds before exhaling. Inhale once more and shake your hands above your head for ten to thirty seconds before exhaling, then relax.

~~~~~

To view a video of this meditation, search for "kundalini meditation for tattva balance beyond stress and duality" on YouTube.

Meditation for a Calm Heart
22 MINUTES

The left side of the body connects to the body's relaxation response in the nerves, while the right side throws us into activity and more alertness. The energy in your body will create anxiousness if it is not settled. When we place the left hand, which is connected to calming the nervous system, on the heart, it helps gather our energy to lower anxiety. The right side, which is our active side, becomes still, and the combination of stillness and gathering the energy in the body creates a relaxation effect. If you are trying to determine what to do, sit in this meditation before you make your decision. It will ensure you're not reacting emotionally. You can start out doing it for just three minutes to get used to it. Next try doing it for three minutes three times with a one-minute rest between each. You can build up to doing the meditation for twenty-two minutes.

> PREPARATION: Your left hand is on your heart center with your fingers pointing right. The fingers are parallel to the ground and not spread. Your right hand is up by your shoulder like you are swearing an oath. Bring your pointer finger and thumb together; the other three fingers on the right hand point up. Your right forearm points straight up and your elbow rests by your side. You are sitting in a cross-legged position with a straight spine and your chin is slightly tucked to bring the back of the neck in line with the spine. Either close your eyes or have them one-tenth open.

> BREATHING TECHNIQUE: Inhale through your nose deeply and slowly, and hold your breath for as long as you can before slowly exhaling. Hold your breath out as long as you can before inhaling. Don't go overboard with the breathing or make it too intense.

> MANTRA: None specified.

> TO FINISH: To end the meditation, take three powerful breaths and then relax.

〜〜〜

To view a video of this meditation, search for "kundalini meditation for a calm heart" on YouTube.

Kriya for Stress or Sudden Shock
11 MINUTES

This meditation can be used right after one experiences something traumatic or for ongoing stress management. The brain is brought into balance to be able to handle a shock and reduce the risk of developing post-traumatic stress. Doing this for forty days in a row will help rebuild your nervous system after a stressful time and can help you feel strong again. After losing someone, experiencing something that puts you into shock, or even going through an emotionally difficult experience, this will help you. Even if you have a lot of stress at home or work, this can help you feel like you can handle it. Stress drains your energy, so you need to build up your reserves.

> PREPARATION: You will sit in a cross-legged position and tuck your chin slightly to line the back of the neck up with the spine. Sit tall so your spine is straight. Your eyes will focus on the tip of the nose. Your elbows are bent and facing out. Hold your hands, palms facing up, just one inch above your belly button. Place your right palm in your left palm and allow your thumbs to touch, then pull the thumbs toward the body.

> BREATHING TECHNIQUE: Take a deep inhale through your nose and then say the mantra below three times in a single breath. You'll find you can do it without letting a lot of air out on each syllable. Continue for eleven minutes.

> MANTRA: *Sat Nam Sat Nam Sat Nam Sat Nam Sat Nam Sat Nam Wahe Guru*

> TO FINISH: Inhale and exhale five times in a row. Inhale and reach up with all your might. Exhale and relax. Inhale and reach up two more times.

~~~

To view a video of this meditation, search for "kundalini yoga meditation with instructions: stress and sudden shock" on YouTube.

Cat-Cow

3 MINUTES

Begin on your hands and knees. Keep your knees hip-distance apart and hands shoulder-distance apart.

As you inhale through your nose, bring your head up and stretch your neck. At the same time, drop your belly button toward the ground as you point the tailbone up.

As you exhale through your nose, arch your spine and pull your chin into your chest. Pull the belly button toward the spine and tuck the tailbone.

Continue this movement at a pace that feels comfortable to you for three minutes. Be sure to breathe powerfully through your nose. To finish, inhale, lifting your head and dropping your belly button toward the ground. Hold the breath in for ten seconds. Then exhale, rounding the back and pulling your chin to your chest. Hold the breath out for ten seconds. Inhale and relax.

~~~~~

To view a video of this, search "kundalini yoga cat cow" on YouTube.

Kundalini Stress Set for Adrenals and Kidneys
11 MINUTES

This set of movements helps to regulate your adrenal glands so you don't get tired and snippy. You'll notice the next day you'll feel very positive and have a smooth energy. This builds up reserve energy that you need to combat stress. Do each of the eleven exercises for a minute and then relax.

> LOTUS MUDRA: Begin by rubbing the palms together. Inhale, bringing the arms straight out to the sides with the wrists bent back at 90 degrees, and exhale, bringing the base of the palms together to form lotus mudra with the thumbs and pinkies of opposite hands touching (see illustration above). Continue moving back and forth with the breath for one minute.

> SIT CROSS-LEGGED AND DO BREATH OF FIRE: Lock your pinkies together and stick the thumbs up, with the

other fingers curled in. Bring your hands in front of the diaphragm where the ribs meet and pull so you feel a stretch across the back as you do breath of fire for one minute through your nose. This is pushing air out of your nose quickly as you snap the navel in and create a rhythm of breathing only through your nose.

SIT CROSS-LEGGED AND DO CANNON BREATH: Pucker your lips and do breath of fire through your mouth. Focus on a quick, powerful exhale as you snap the navel in and let the inhale happen naturally. Continue for one minute and then inhale and focus on your spine for five seconds. Exhale.

SIT CROSS-LEGGED AND CHANT: Keep your eyes wide open and bring your left arm behind you, placing the back of your hand on your back. Reach the right arm straight forward and with fingers together bend the wrist up 60 degrees. Chant *Har* (which sounds like "hud") as you snap the navel each time for one minute.

BODY DROPS: Sitting in a cross-legged position, lift your body by placing your hands next to your hips on the ground. Inhale as you lift yourself and then exhale as you drop yourself. Keep the back teeth clenched so you do not bite your tongue. Continue for one minute.

SIT CROSS-LEGGED WITH POWERFUL DEEP BREATHING: Now you will cleanse with a long, deep, powerful breath as you place the left palm facing the diaphragm so the wrist is centered with the body and press the palm of your right hand into your left wrist but don't touch the body with the hands. Continue breathing deeply through the nose as you gaze down for one minute.

FRONT STRETCH WITH STRAIGHT SPINE: Straighten your legs out in front of you and bring your arms straight forward with fingers curled and your thumbs pointing straight up. Lean forward as you exhale out of your nose and inhale through your nose as you lean back. Keep your arms parallel to the ground and continue for one minute.

LIFT YOUR PELVIS: Lie on your back and bend your knees so your heels touch your backside. If you can, hold your ankles. Inhale through the nose and lift your pelvis. Exhale out of the nose and lower your pelvis. Continue for one minute.

CAT-COW MODIFIED: Come onto your hands and knees and inhale, lifting your chin and arching the back slightly as you bring your left leg straight back. Exhale and bring your left knee to your chin as you round the back. Switch sides. Continue for one minute.

SIT ON YOUR HEELS: Sit on your heels and bring your forearms to the ground so your palms are together and your thumbs point up. Inhale, stretch forward over your palms, and exhale as you sit back. Keep your chin up the entire time to help stretch the lower back. Continue for one minute.

ROLL ON YOUR BACK: Hug your knees to your chest and roll back and forth, breathing through your nose, for one minute. Roll along the full length of the spine to massage the muscles that line the spine.

RELAX: Have a glass of water and relax on your back.

~~~~~~

To view a video of this, search "kundalini yoga stress set for the adrenals and kidneys" on YouTube.

Vitality

Spinal Flexes
3 MINUTES

This will help open the heart chakra and awaken your own energy and vitality.

Sit in a cross-legged position and hold your shins. Inhale through your nose as you stretch your chest forward and lift the sternum, bringing an arch to the spine. Exhale through the nose and round the back, tilting the pelvis backward and bringing the navel toward the spine. The head remains neutral so that it doesn't bob back and forth, and you isolate the movement in the spine. Think of stretching the spine and chest.

Continue rigorously breathing and move faster as your spine warms up. Avoid this if you have herniated discs or disc problems. Continue for three minutes. To finish, pull the heart forward and inhale, holding for ten seconds. Exhale and relax.

~~~~~~~

To view a video of this, search "kundalini yoga spinal flex" on YouTube.

Strengthening the Aura
7 MINUTES

This is a powerful set of exercises that will attract love and bring you confidence by strengthening the electromagnetic field around your body. You may find it challenging at first, but stick with it for forty days and you'll find that because of the intense aerobic breathing, the muscles develop quickly. There are three parts to this sequence. This will help you attract positive experiences while repelling negative ones.

Start in downward-facing dog, which is basically a triangle pose (see top row of opposite illustration). Your hands are as wide as your shoulders and feet as wide as your hips. Lift the right leg and keep it straight and do pushups in this position, exhaling through your nose as you lower your chest and inhaling as you raise back up. Continue for one minute and then repeat the same thing on the other side. If you can't add the push-ups yet, try to hold downward facing dog with your leg up on each side.

Next, sit in a cross-legged position with a straight spine and bring your left arm out in front of you straight as if you're grasping a pole. Bring your right arm straight forward under your left and wrap your right hand around the left. Inhale through your nose, lifting your arms to a 60-degree angle, and exhale through your nose back to shoulder height (see middle row of facing illustration). Continue this pumping for two minutes.

Finally, bring your arms straight out in front of your face six inches apart with your palms facing each other. Inhale and bring your arms back at a downward angle (see bottom row of facing illustration), then exhale powerfully and bring them back to the original position. Breathe powerfully for three minutes, keeping a rhythm.

~~~~~~

To view a video of this, search "kundalini yoga to strengthen the aura" on YouTube.

Quick Exercises to Improve Vitality & Concentration

Compression of the spine, misalignment, and compression of the life nerve reduce our ability to concentrate and use our mental ability. These two simple exercises can help you with each of these things.

Frog Exercise
3–5 MINUTES

Squat so you are on your toes with heels together and knees wide. Bring your fingertips to the ground with your head up (see illustration, left). Lift your hips, bringing your head to your knees as you inhale through your nose and straighten your legs (illustration, right). Keep your heels up. Exhale and return to the original position. Do this twenty-six times.

To view a video of this, search "kundalini yoga frogs" on YouTube.

Life Nerve Stretch
3 MINUTES

Sit with your legs together out in front of you. Reach for your big toes with your pointer and middle finger and wrap them around your big toes, pressing your thumbs into your big toenails. Elongate your spine and then lean forward, still holding your toes. Stay in the position for three minutes and breathe long and deep breaths through your nose.

To view a video of this, search "kundalini life nerve stretch" on YouTube.

An Inspiring Story

One of the most life-changing kriyas I have worked with came at a very unique time. I was living in Los Angeles and used to hike in Runyon Canyon near my house. I was on one of my daily hikes when my heart started racing in a panic. I felt like someone in my family was not safe, and it was an overwhelming feeling that made me stop. I am usually calm, and feeling like that had only happened once when I drank too much concentrated cold brew coffee on accident. This seemed strange, so I emailed my kundalini teacher right there from my phone, asking her to pray for my family member and envision them as being safe. People from all over the world ask for her prayers and she genuinely takes them seriously. She has been praying for people, teaching, and working with kundalini energy for many years, and her energy is very powerful. She emailed me back that she was praying and suggested I do the ancestral karma–clearing kriya, which I did when I got home from my hike.

That night I didn't know what was about to happen. I woke up the next day and found out a family member was in the hospital. He had been robbed and stabbed by the masked clown gang that had been terrorizing Southern California. He said the assailants had tried to stab him in the chest, but he had blocked the knife and was hit in the arm instead, which probably saved his life.

The kriya that I had done was to help not only clear my own ancestral karma but also to help family members. I thought it was interesting that

I received and performed the kriya before such a traumatic, life threatening event. I decided to continue doing the kriya daily. In that time, the relationships, careers, health, and emotional well-being of many family members dramatically improved while I was doing this on my own each day. Major positive changes kept occurring for the next eight months as I kept it up. Then I was invited to a wedding across the country and was to be staying with a family I didn't know. I didn't do the kriya daily for the first time in months. Suddenly, at the end of the week, I received a call that a family member who had been doing well had suddenly taken a bad turn. I thought it was also interesting that this was the first downturn since I had started doing the kriya.

I also taught this kriya to a good friend of mine who was seriously concerned for his family member's health. They were working a job that was causing them pain and felt they had no other option. As my friend did this kriya with the intention of helping his family member, he had no idea how it might help. Shortly after doing the kriya for a week or two, he received word that his family member was able to leave their job because they had been awarded funds that covered their expenses, and they hadn't known they were entitled to them. It was out of the blue and seemed like a miracle. It was interesting how this all seemed to happen just after my friend started putting his energy into helping his family member out of sheer love and compassion.

What is a mantra? Mantra is two words: man and tra. Man means mind. Tra means the heat of life. Ra means sun. So, mantra is a powerful combination of words which, if recited, takes the vibratory effect of each of your molecules into the Infinity of the Cosmos. That is called "Mantra."

Yogi Bhajan

5

Chanting

Prayer and chanting have been used universally as a method to enhance spiritual connection and develop an altered state to connect to unified consciousness. There are quite a few names for the use of sound in a spiritual manner, including chant, recitation, affirmation, mantra, prayer, incantation, spell, and naad. Let's look at the commonalities in the definitions of these words briefly.

CHANT: a repeated rhythmic phrase

RECITATION: the act of repeating something aloud from memory

AFFIRMATION: the action or process of affirming something

MANTRA: a sacred utterance

PRAYER: a solemn request for help or an expression of thanks addressed to God or an object of worship

INCANTATION: a series of words said as a magic spell or charm

SPELL: a form of words used as an incantation or magical charm

NAAD: the cosmic sound or vibrations of the cosmos

We know that prayers are said universally throughout the world, and those who are more science-based often choose to use affirmations because there is an effect when they repeat something on their energy. The mantras chanted by yogis are no different than a prayer said by a Catholic or a recitation said by a Buddhist. They are all sound currents that have a wavelength and interact with energy in the universe.

The interesting thing that most cultures share about sound is that they can use it silently. Prayers are often thought to oneself and are still considered powerful. In the yogic tradition, mantra can be heard, said out loud, or said mentally for the same effect. We can hear sound in our mind when we say things mentally. One of the most well-known and widely used mantras is *Om.* When chanted out loud, this sound vibrates parts of the body that activate the upper chakras and help one connect to a peaceful, loving frequency. The kundalini yogis prefer to chant *Ong* because it resonates in the head, strongly vibrating the pineal gland. The mantra is sometimes chanted or written as *Aum,* which still brings vibration from the heart to the head. If you think of the body like a guitar, the sound is resonating in the cavities, activating the energy centers there to create specific frequencies, just like notes of a guitar string that shift when the vibration is truncated with different frets. We are playing our chakras as we chant with different sounds.

Ong

11 MINUTES

Chant this for eleven minutes daily in a monotone voice. The sound resonates in the back of the nose and the mouth stays open. It will vibrate the sixth chakra, the third eye chakra, and you may feel your nose itch from the vibration. It helps your thyroid and vibrates the central channel, sushumna. For those with physical injuries who cannot do movement or breathwork, this is a great chant to help awaken and raise kundalini. This will help you reach a state of bliss.

Tibetan Buddhist Mantras

Tibetan Buddhism has friendly ties with modern kundalini yoga practitioners of the West. The links to kriya, raja, and laya yoga trace back to similar origins in the Himalayan Mountains, where they share a common border. One very valuable asset of understanding Tibetan Buddhist's approach to meditation and mantras is that the step-by-step process of first training the brain to be still helps one, through contemplation, to then remove the neurotic patterns of the mind that block one from experiencing expanded states of consciousness. The great emphasis on reciting mantras in Tibetan Buddhism reveals the very real and large benefit one gets from being aware of the mind and able to calm it. While there are less well-known movement practices as well in Tibetan yoga, the focus on emptying the mind helps elucidate the mental prep work that can allow one to use breathwork and movement to then master energy, as many stories of Tibetan Buddhist monks exemplify.

The low self-esteem suffered by many in the West is very uncommon in the practice of Tibetan Buddhism because of the renunciation of value of worldly acquisitions. There are different lineages of Tibetan Buddhism that include different levels of physical training, but the use of mantras is heavy in each. Perhaps the Western mind's approach to things is influenced by the culture of trying to be the best, get there the fastest, and become a powerful leader, as we are trained to do in school. But this can lead us to practice the physical aspects of kundalini yoga more than the more subtle aspects of sound and meditation, which are where the ego is stripped of its ability to wreak havoc on our happiness.

The problems of kundalini awakening where people push too fast may be from them having the wrong intention or no intention in their practice and really just seeking to find a sense of confidence. We must humble ourselves to be able to reach a state of enlightenment, and due to the highly egotistical nature of Western culture (particularly American), it is highly recommended that the physically aggressive exercises be used less than the calming meditations so that one learns to slow and dissect their own thought patterns. The breathing techniques of kundalini yoga are very effective in that they help clear the subconscious to help one get to a higher vibration state and clear the slate for about twenty-four hours, but if you don't keep up with your daily practice, you can quickly fall back into the egoic patterns that will still be there if your subconscious mind is left to its own devices.

Insecurities are loud. Confidence is quiet.

Sanskrit Mantras

Sanskrit is the language used for Hindu mantras as well as some Buddhist mantras. The mantras have a meaning that it is intended for the practitioner to focus on. One famous mantra is *Om Mani Padme Hum,* which helps induce a state of compassion for yourself and others. Mantras are used to help retrain the mind to overcome fear, negative thought patterns, and self-chastising thoughts. They scrub the mind but also, over time, help to create new patterns that are more based on kindness and a deeper truth of your spiritual nature to help you tune into it. The use of mantras in yoga classes in the West is not very common.

The word *namaste* is often said at the end of class, but the chanting in classes can leave some feeling confused or just embarrassed because it's rare that the teacher explains the chant, and students are just expected to catch on eventually. The emphasis on mantras in the West is significantly underrated because, to be honest, yoga teachers are not taught much about them. If they do incorporate them, they do not tend to spend a lot of time on them due to the demand paying students have to "get a workout." Given this information of how mantra has been fairly nonexistent in the popularized versions of yoga in the West, we can see why someone new to kundalini yoga may consider them less valuable than a movement where they know they are doing something to their body. A deeper understanding of the energetic power of words and sound is necessary to truly grasp the technology of a mantra and why it is not a part of the yogic lifestyle to overlook.

Gurmukhi Mantras

While many people think that it would be just as valuable to chant the mantra in English, these mantras were designed to move energy through the body based on where they resonate in the body. Therefore, knowing the literal translation is not necessary for the mantra to move energy and change the practitioner's frequency. The intention, however, is powerful as well, so knowing what the mantra is intended for does amplify the use of it.

According to Yogi Bhajan:

> Every element in the universe is in a constant state of vibration manifested to us as light, sound, and energy. The human senses perceive only a fraction of the infinite range of vibration, so it is difficult to comprehend that the Word mentioned in the Bible is actually the totality of vibration which underlies and sustains all creation. A person can tune his or her own consciousness into the awareness of that totality with the use of a mantra. By vibrating in rhythm with the breath to a particular sound that is proportional to the creative sound, or sound current, one can expand one's sensitivity to the entire spectrum of vibration. It is similar to striking a note on a stringed instrument. In other words, as you vibrate, the universe vibrates with you (*The Aquarian Teacher*, 66).

One of the focal points of chanting mantras in kundalini yoga is keeping a rhythm so that you get in tune with the pulse of the universe. Pronouncing the sounds correctly is also important. You wouldn't play an A in replace of a G in a song and get the same result, and just as these mantras are coded to unlock specific frequencies, the note must be played. When you vibrate the mantra, you match the frequency of the desired state and join with that consciousness to perceive the energetic universe. The mantras vibrate certain parts of the face and interact with the meridian system at the roof of the mouth. The mantras are like a computer code for the meridian points on the upper palate, where you can call into the universe.

Before reciting the mantras, it is a good idea to look them up online and listen to the correct pronunciation. There are multiple versions freely available on YouTube.

Mantras to Use to Lower Stress

Mantras are used to send the mind in a specific direction and develop a certain emotional state. The more frequently you use them, the more you can reach the desired state. Mantras are great for busy people because they can be listened to during our daily activities such as driving, sleeping, working out, cooking, etc. Mantras can either be chanted, listened to, or recited mentally. Using a mantra for a minimum of forty days in a row will help you change your brain patterns and experience the effects they are reported to have. You can find most of these mantras online or through any music platform by a variety of artists.

> LONG SAT NAM: This calls your awareness to the true nature of who you are to forget about the petty things. *Sat* means truth, and *Nam* means identity. Take a deep inhale and elongate the words, chanting in a monotone voice *Saaaat Naaam*. Doing this for just one or three minutes can calm you down.

> ANG SANG WAHE GURU: This mantra is used to cut negativity or disperse negative energy around you. Raise your vibration quickly by mentally reciting this mantra or listening to it. This mantra means "The dynamic, loving

energy of the Infinite Source of All is dancing within every cell of me." Try chanting it mentally throughout the day and notice how you feel.

AAD GURAY NAMEH: This is a protective mantra that is a bit longer. Yogis use this anytime they want to protect something. This is great for empathic people who can unconsciously take on stress from the environment. The full mantra is *Aad Guray Nameh, Jugad Guray Nameh, Sat Guray Nameh, Siri Guru Devay Nameh.* The translation means "I bow to the primal Guru (guiding consciousness who takes us to God-Realization), I bow to wisdom through the ages, I bow to True Wisdom, I bow to the great, unseen wisdom." You can visualize protective energy on all four sides of you or anything you want to protect as you say it three times.

Mantras to Use to Overcome Addiction

SA TA NA MA: This mantra is used to transform you and connect you with a calm and infinite loving energy. If you need to change your life, this will help you physically and emotionally heal as well as bring balance back into your life. *Sa* is infinity, *Ta* is life, *Na* means death, and *Ma* is rebirth.

ONG NAMO GURU DEV NAMO: This mantra means "I call upon divine wisdom" or "To the great creative force, I welcome you." This helps you connect to infinite wisdom and attune to higher vibrations. It can be chanted three times to tune into spiritual vibrations. This is chanted before kundalini yoga classes to tune into the golden chain of teachers.

WAHE GURU: This is about moving darkness into light. This elevates the spirit and is an exclamation of bliss. It can be chanted mentally while walking around or going throughout your day to keep a rhythm, to keep the thoughts directed and positive, and to avoid negativity.

Mantras to Use to Open to Love

HAMI HAM BRAHM HAM: This mantra will invoke your inner light. It means "We are God, we are God." It helps you hear what you are saying and realize how you create energy when you speak. Many people do not understand what they say, and it negatively affects their relationships. You can create love by speaking through the use of this mantra. This mantra works on the heart center.

LONG EK ONG KARS: The full mantra is *Ek Ong Kar Sat Nam Siri Wahe Guru.* It helps raise your vibration and manifest what you focus on for the next twenty-four hours. It clears and charges your chakras. It is called "the greatest divine key" and connects you to divine consciousness. Use it to relate to the soul of a person instead of their lower consciousness.

GURU GIATRI: The full mantra is *Gobinday, Mukunday, Udaray, Aparay, Hariang, Kariang, Nirnamay, Akamay.* It purifies your aura and removes past errors. It means "Sustaining, liberating, enlightening, infinite, destroying, creating, nameless, desireless." It works on the heart center to develop patience and compassion. It helps bring mental balance as well.

An Inspiring Story

During my first kundalini yoga teacher training in Santa Monica, California, we were given a kriya to do for ninety days. We were given *Sa Re Sa Sa*, which is simple in that you just sit there and say the mantra for thirty-one minutes a day with a specific arm and hand configuration. I wasn't particularly excited about this because I felt like it was one of the less powerful ones. I assumed the really physically challenging ones would offer the best results. This was more about my own associations to physical exercise than based in a true understanding of the wavelengths of thoughts, sound, and energy. This particular meditation/kriya is said to bring power to our words and make people take us more seriously.

I really didn't have high expectations of this kriya, but the results were astounding. I found that the emails I wrote were giving me tremendous results. I was being taken seriously, and it was bringing prosperity. It was as if I really needed to be careful what I asked for because I was suddenly flooded with opportunity. I can absolutely attest that this is a powerful mantra that, when done consistently, does bring a power to your words.

A few years later, I found out I needed to have surgery for a hernia. I would be out of work, and the timing was really not ideal because I had just moved to San Diego to study one-hand handstands with the top hand-balancing coach in the world. I had arranged my life around being able to study with this coach, and suddenly I needed to have surgery and would be in recovery for weeks, if not months. I was determined to speed up the recovery process, but because they were cutting through layers of my stomach muscles, I couldn't do movements or breathwork. This is when I really found the healing power of mantra. I knew the healing mantra *Ra Ma Da Sa* was used to send healing and to receive it, so I played the mantra after my surgery as much as I could. I remembered my teacher saying that sometimes you don't have the energy to move and sometimes all you can do is hit play and let the mantras work on your energy. Within five weeks I was back at the circus center, training handstands, contortion, and trapeze without issue. I attribute my fast recovery to using the mantra, which helped me stay in a positive state and focus on a positive outcome.

*What is a meditative mind? With
all the pressure on your mind of this
whole world, you keep yourself calm.*

Yogi Bhajan

6

Meditation

Meditation is generally considered a practice of sitting in stillness. However, different systems around the world have created moving meditations as well. There are walking meditation practices, prostration meditations, and meditations with repetitive movements or statements. To meditate, people use drums, breathing, mantras, and certain body positions. We see many cultures also incorporating nature into meditation to help deepen the state. We have all seen movies and heard about someone going out into nature to find clarity and answers. What is it about being alone in nature that helps us find this clarity? Why are stillness or repetitive movements able to help us reach a state of enlightenment?

When we meditate, we try to get the body to feel at ease. Often breathing will relax the nerves so that we feel that sense of peace and the tension in our body dissipates. This may seem to contradict meditations that involve movement such as hitting a drum, walking, or dancing, but the altered state of mind can be accessed by giving the mind a task so that it is not running around looking for problems to solve. When we can forget about trying to weed through all the thoughts the mind is having, we can start to experience an altered state of consciousness. It's as if giving the mind a break from computing is the golden ticket to the door of bliss. Even our little finger tapping or pen clicking can subconsciously help us think more clearly or allow us to order our mind. You may realize that you naturally stop trying to fix or solve a problem when you feel frustrated and do something like cleaning or cooking, which allows the mind to shut off so you can get a fresh perspective.

Yogis make a clear distinction in levels of consciousness and work to understand the mind and the consciousness that essentially exists beyond the mind. The mind will continue to run—that is a constant; it is up to us to train it to work for us. Most of us don't really differentiate between the mind, body, and spirit because we are so engaged in what we see, hear, and experience in the external world. The practice of becoming more aware of the internal world and the patterns of the mind is greatly empowering, and throughout history this process of meditation, the internal work, has been prevalent in the world. Of course, we have developed different words, practices, and methods of meditating, but one key truth stands out: meditation is a vital part of the path to enlightenment.

A Key Universal Path to Enlightenment

To expand upon the notion that meditation is one of the universal practices of raising kundalini, let's observe some cultures around the world and their meditation practices.

THE NAGA: This group of naked yogis in India who cover themselves in ashes is one of the groups of ascetics still very much alive in the world today. While modern Westerners may not understand their worldview or lifestyle, these yogis practice a life of anonymity, meditation, and spiritual development of their own accord. They live primarily in nature or very simply so they can meditate and perform holy rituals. Their devout spiritual practices are geared to connect them to the spiritual so they do not fear death nor require material possessions to be happy. This group, said to have started 2,500 years ago, is still seen as the holy men of India. While Western culture strives to achieve status through accumulation of wealth, in this country status can be seen in a new light as a path of spiritual development.

THE BRAHMINS: Considered the highest social class in India. This refers to the priest class, and often they are also in government, teaching, and writing positions. It's interesting to note that the highest positions of power are required to have the utmost purity, a strong spiritual practice and study, as well as education of spirituality. Their role as priests also gives them the ability to be landowners and wealthy, but the service they provide is very spiritually focused. Traditionally, their day starts and is centered around meditation and meditative practices.

NATIVE AMERICAN CEREMONIAL HEALING: Native Americans have a unique healing ritual where the medicine man or woman calls the community together to meditate through a variety of means, including dancing, praying, and singing, to help someone heal. The meditation allows for healing energy to be joined to bring more powerful energy to the afflicted person. These ceremonies can last for long periods of time. It is also common to run at dawn to help keep spiritual energy strong, and living in harmony with and close to nature is emphasized as well.

CATHOLIC MEDITATION RITUALS: The Catholic religion has a large emphasis on daily meditative practices such as Mass or prayer. Reciting prayers is a repetitive form of meditation used to connect one's consciousness to the divine and overcome the lower mind that gets attached to the world and pulled away from the peace of a spiritual state. The emphasis on daily devotion is a cornerstone of this faith, as rosaries are used to recite prayers and prayers are memorized to create a tool box one can pull from for inspiration.

AFRICAN DRUMMING: The repetitive action of drumming is seen in many cultures as a meditative practice. African drumming is not reserved for a select few; it is seen as a way of life and a way to help encourage dancing, which rids the community of negativity. Many African cultures use dance and drums to come together to bring healing and restore the spiritual connection of the community.

TIBETAN BUDDHIST PROSTRATION AND PRAYER WHEELS: Tibetan Buddhists use a very specific type of prostration to help purify the mind. It is sometimes done in the home, by a holy place, or on a journey to a holy place. This lying down also includes a specific hand gesture with the palms together and the thumbs tucked in. Another form of meditation is the spinning of prayer wheels while walking around holy places. This repetitive practice gives the mind something to do so it can stop going all over the place and one's consciousness can merge with the infinite.

Meditation to Raise Kundalini

In kundalini yoga, all of the meditations work to raise kundalini, so it's not necessary to obsess over finding the right one. While certain meditations also have other benefits and purposes, when done properly, the continual practice of any of them will help in the stimulation and raising of kundalini. If one is sloppy in their posture, pronunciation, breathing, visualization, mudras, or angles, the benefits will diminish. The accuracy of the meditation is like putting in a formula that will get a desired result. The proper body locks and eye positions, as well as the way the mouth and tongue move, are all significant, which is why studying with a kundalini yoga master is so beneficial. We do not have someone reminding us of these minutia when we are meditating at home, and that is why people prefer to live close to a meditation center in the kundalini yoga community. There's a lot to focus on to not get sloppy and to stay motivated to do it every day. Being in a group while meditating is also more powerful because the energy of the group joins and helps deepen meditation.

Of course, each kundalini yoga practitioner and teacher works on their personal meditations at home and in their personal practice, they will have to develop their own self-discipline. Once you begin practicing, you will get into the habit of it and it will feel as natural as brushing your teeth each morning, which is something you do without thinking. If you do some of the meditations that directly stimulate kundalini energy in this chapter, you can essentially put yourself on a faster road to experience this universal state of enlightenment. If you are combining them with daily yoga sets (kriyas) and breathwork, healthy eating, herbs for vitality, hydration, and tools to deepen meditation, your kundalini will start to rise even quicker. Of course, each person has different stress, toxins, subconscious blocks, and time constraints, so there is no guaranteed amount of time that you will get there, but knowing how to get there is the first step, and knowing many people just like you do get there is inspiration.

You do not have to be born into a certain family to practice kundalini. You are not excluded from it if you have done drugs, gone to jail, been to rehab, or cheated on a partner. There is no shaming of your past in this system, merely helpful tools to help break the cycles of self-sabotage in order to align your energy and awaken your potential to be happy. The man who is most well-known for bringing this to the United States, Yogi Bhajan, arrived in the 1960s during the time when drugs were sweeping the nation. People were desperately seeking some sense of peace and a deeper connection to life in response to the

Vietnam War, which lasted from 1955–1975. Yogi Bhajan saw how the culture was struggling with addiction and knew what they were seeking could also be found through the less-known kundalini yoga practices of India (you can find more comparisons of the effects of drugs and the effects of kundalini yoga in chapter 7). This type of yoga was practiced by the royals and reserved for them because it has such profound and quick effects. However, breaking with tradition, Yogi Bhajan decided to provide this to people who he saw were suffering mentally, emotionally, and physically. It was said that anyone who exposed this secret practice to the public would be dead within a year, and Yogi Bhajan did get very sick but didn't die.

He was also the head of the Sikh religion (which has different sects) but made it clear in his teachings that, first of all, he did not want disciples, and secondly, that you do not need to be religious to practice kundalini yoga. He was a charismatic leader who pushed himself to master yoga by the age of seventeen. He was able to develop very rare abilities, and students of his who are still alive tell stories of him teaching students to levitate. His students shared experiences with him where he was able to remote view, use extreme psychic vision, and even be able to control the element of water. Many of his students developed a number of these gifts and continue to pass on the steps to unlock them.

It is important to note that one does not need to follow any one person because following the teachings is and should remain the focus since the ancient system of kundalini yoga works with the technology of the body, mind, and spirit.

Using Meditation Beads

Meditation beads are a meditative tool used throughout the world to assist in directing the mind and achieving a connection to divine consciousness. The use of meditation beads in Asia began as a result of spiritual necessity. Because they had familial financial obligations, many who could not afford to join the life of meditation in a Buddhist ashram used the free resource of seeds strung together on a necklace to create a way to repeat mantras. This was the beginning of both the practice of the rosary and what many people know as mala beads, which today can be made of crystals.

The use of beads to invoke a spiritual energy is prevalent in many cultures, and you will usually find beads are a part of spiritual practices. They not only remind the wearer of their quest to remain peaceful, but they actually help the person count their recitations. The design of mala beads, which have one bigger bead, helps a person know when to stop their recitations and is similar in the rosary design, which has a cross. The actual beads themselves are also able to hold energy as a power object and become something that helps induce a deeper state of meditation, just as a sacred place begins to fill with a high-vibration resonance over time and use. Certain energies of high-vibration people can be imbued into the beads to help imprint the cellular or molecular structure to raise the vibration of the person wearing them. This practice of wearing spiritual jewelry is not just to indicate a spiritual fashion preference; it has energetic properties that are seen to help one in their lifestyle of raising consciousness.

My book *Modern Guide to Meditation Beads* explores the use of meditation beads in depth and covers how to use and make them.

Early Morning Meditation

Kundalini yogis rise before the sun, just as many people in other cultures do, to meditate. Muslims pray before sunrise, and Buddhist practitioners say before sunrise is the best time for meditation. While the earth is still and there is quiet energy, you can set your own energy for the day. The kundalini yogis say that the angle the energy is to the sun at this time amplifies the meditation, making it much more powerful. It is interesting that so many cultures promote pre-sunrise meditation, and it has been practiced across cultures for so long. If they are in class, kundalini yogis generally do a light yoga set, recite mantras, and relax while the teacher plays the gong; if they are at home, they start their practice with a cold shower (see chapter 9). They also tend to go to bed early in order to do this practice.

Mudras

Mudras are specific placements of the hands and fingers. Mudras are used in martial arts training, Tibetan Buddhism, hatha yoga, and kundalini yoga. The planetary energies are the focal point of mudras in yoga. Certain fingers seem to join certain aspects of the brain's circuitry to activate thinking processes. Communication is the goal of buddhi mudra, where the pinky finger and thumb press together, while wisdom is the goal of gyan mudra, where the thumb and pointer finger meet. Buddhi mudra is said to stimulate the Mercury energy in our consciousness; Mercury is the planet of thinking and communication. Gyan mudra is said to stimulate the Jupiter energy, which helps our mind expand.

THUMB: Sun (Ego)

POINTER FINGER: Jupiter (Wisdom)

MIDDLE FINGER: Saturn (Patience)

RING FINGER: Uranus (Energy)

PINKY: Mercury (Communication)

The yogis have done an excellent job mapping the flow of consciousness in the brain in response to certain movements and positions. When you see a little detail in a kundalini yoga meditation that says "cover the thumbs" or something that seems minor because it is a simple finger placement, it may make a huge difference on the meditation's overall effect on your energy. For example, the meditation *Sa Re Sa Sa* helps one's words become powerful and taken seriously, and it utilizes the buddhi mudra. It is essentially creating a new brain pattern using the power of sound and mudra.

Meditation with Magic Mantra
3–31 MINUTES

Interestingly, the most powerful mantra in kundalini yoga uses a mudra for meditation with it. This mantra is said to move you beyond duality and beyond obstacles. In kundalini yoga it is stressed that this mantra be used in a very sacred manner. Always chant this mantra and all mantras with a positive, pure intention. Always chant it in a reverent space and in a reverent way. Chant for three minutes to start and eventually work up to thirty-one minutes. It will bring you to a very elevated state and make your mind very powerful. Remember these are most effective when done for a minimum of forty days in a row.

PREPARATION: Before chanting this mantra, chant the Mul Mantra or the Mangala Charn Mantra to prepare your energy for it. The Mul Mantra is known to help make us aware of our purpose and the means to live it if chanted daily for eleven minutes. Here is the Mul Mantra; many recordings online have it recited eleven times to music you can listen to (Gurunam Singh's version is nice).

MUL MANTRA: *Ek Ong Kaar, Sat Naam, Karataa Purakh Nirbho, Nirvair, Akaal Moorat, Ajoonee, Saibhang, Gur Prasaad. Jap! Aad Such, Jugaad Such, Hai Bhee Such, Naanak Hosee Bhee Such*

MANGALA CHARN MANTRA: Also known as the protective mantra, this is chanted at least three times in a row while visualizing protective energy surrounding you on all four sides in a clockwise direction: *Aad Guray Nameh, Jugaad Guray Nameh, Sat Guray Nameh, Siri Guru Dayvay Nameh*

DIRECTIONS: Sit in a cross-legged position with a straight spine. Have your elbows at your sides and cup your palms so they make a shallow cup in front of your heart. Keep the pinkies together with as little gap as possible. Your eyes will be closed, looking at the palms in your mind's eye. Your hands are held up at about 30 degrees from the elbows and thumbs stick out to the side.

MANTRA: *Ek Ong Kar, Sat Gur Prasad* (said in a monotone voice once about every four to five seconds)

TO FINISH: Relax the mudra.

~~~

To view a video of this meditation, search for "kundalini meditation with magic mantra" on YouTube.

Meditation for Supernatural Powers
11–31 MINUTES

This meditation was said to be used by the Egyptians for supernatural powers. It is a secret and sacred teaching. It is said that it will show you the power of your breath. Start with five minutes and work up to eleven. You can work up to thirty-one minutes, but eleven is very powerful.

PREPARATION: Sit in a cross-legged position with a straight spine. Your eyes will remain partially closed, looking at the tip of the nose. Your forearms come together and you make fists with the butts of the hands touching and the fingernails touching. The thumbs do not touch and point away from each other. The hands are about a foot from the chin. Breathe in slowly through the nose and hold as long as you can while mentally reciting the mantra. Then breathe all the way out through your nose and hold your breath out as long as you can while mentally reciting the mantra.

MANTRA: *Aad Sach, Jugaad Sach, Heibhee Sach, Naanak Hosee Bhee Sach*

TO FINISH: Inhale and hold the breath. Reach your arms up and stretch your spine. Exhale. Do that twice more and then relax.

~~~~~~

To find a video of this, search for "kundalini to balance the right and left hemispheres of the brain and Kriya for supernatural powers" on YouTube. Note the meditation is around the sixty-minute mark.

Meditation to Experience Deathlessness
11–31 MINUTES

Also called Pran Bandha, this meditation helps you merge with the supreme you and feel that God is within you. It helps you link to the energy that is infinite. It shows you another timeless dimension of yourself and life, which helps us not be controlled by attachments in the physical world. This helps you merge with the pranic body, which never dies, and it helps you become one with the creative magnetic field of consciousness. To experience the desired results, practice this for at least forty days in a row.

~~~

A good mantra version to use is *Pavan Guru* by Gurunam Singh on YouTube.

PREPARATION: Sit in a cross-legged position with a straight spine and a slight neck lock. Your hands can be in gyan mudra, resting on your knees. Listen to the mantra for a minute, feeling it vibrate in your cells, and then join in. Roll your eyes up slightly with the lids closed and focus at the third eye. Do the meditation for eleven to thirty-one minutes.

MANTRA: *Pavan Pavan Pavan Pavan,*
Para Paraa, Pavan Guroo,
Pavan Guroo, Wha-Hay Guroo,
Wha-Hay Guroo, Pavan Guroo

TO FINISH: Relax the mudra.

Meditation for Self-Blessing Guidance by Intuition
11–31 MINUTES

This can seem challenging, but you'll be surprised how much strength the breath gives you. Your arms will be in the upper arc line of your body, and this will help activate the crown chakra. This meditation also activates the pineal and pituitary glands to turn on the third eye and seat of the soul, where intuition comes through visions. This can help you make decisions and helps you determine what is real intuition or just imagination. It is great for guidance and gives you the persistence to live for your soul's purpose. You'll do the meditation for eleven minutes to start. Eventually you can work up to twenty-two and then thirty-one minutes. To achieve the results, practice this for at least forty days in a row.

PREPARATION: Sit in a cross-legged position with a straight spine and a slight neck lock. Keep your eyes only one-tenth open during the meditation. Your arms are above your head in an arc with your palms facing down and hands about seven inches above the head. There is about a foot between your hands. The thumbs hang down away from the other fingers. You will breathe in for eight strokes through your nose as you recite the mantra mentally. Breathe out for eight strokes through your nose as you recite the mantra mentally. Hold your breath out for sixteen beats as you recite the mantra mentally.

MANTRA: *Saa Taa Naa Maa*

FINISH: Inhale, holding your arms up high and reaching them backward. Drop your head back as well so you can look up. Feel as if you're stretching the lower back, spine, and neck. Exhale, letting the arms down. Repeat two more times.

~~~~~~

To view a video of this, search for "kundalini yoga meditation for self-blessing and guidance by intuition" on YouTube.

Laya Yoga Kundalini Mantra
11–31 MINUTES

To achieve the results this meditation can offer, practice it at least forty days in a row. Then it will etch into your subconscious the true spiritual self and allow you to align your life with that spiritual identity. It allows you to experience your higher consciousness and soul. This will help you get clear with your purpose and remove distractions that keep you from living your purpose. This directly awakens your kundalini and helps you align your willpower with the greater good. For anyone lucky enough to come across this powerful meditation in their lifetime, it will unlock great expansion. Focus on positive thoughts and positive energy throughout the day when you use this meditation. The sound itself will connect you to the great creative force of the universe. It will give you intuition and healing power.

> PREPARATION: Sit in a cross-legged position with a light neck lock. Your eyes will be closed; focus on the brow. Hands rest on the knees in gyan mudra. Pull your navel in lightly on *Ek*. At the end of each line of the mantra, pull the diaphragm up and in powerfully, which will make the "uh" sound. Relax the stomach on the line *Hay Guru*. Visualize energy spiraling up three and a half times as you say the mantra from the base of the spine up and out the top of the head. The spin direction is counterclockwise, as if there were a clock on the floor.

> MANTRA: *Ek Ong Kaar-uh, Sa Ta Na Ma-uh, Siree Wa-uh, Hay Guru*

> TO FINISH: Inhale, exhale. Relax.

~~~

To view a video of this, search "kundalini yoga laya yoga meditation" on YouTube.

Ganpati Kriya Meditation
15 MINUTES

This meditation helps remove obstacles. It works energetically to remove blocks that come from your own karma. This can help you energetically release attachments to the past and remove negative fate while also helping you create good actions and energy in the present. It also helps the projection of your future to help you be prosperous and fulfilled. It can give you great wisdom. Practice it for a minimum of forty days to get the desired result.

> PREPARATION: Sit in a cross-legged position with a straight spine and a slight neck lock. Your eyes will be one-tenth open, and your mental focus should be at the third eye point. For the first eleven minutes, you will chant in a monotone voice. You will chant the entire mantra on one breath, and on each syllable connect the thumb to another finger. So, for *Saa*, connect the thumb to the pointer finger. For *Taa*, connect the thumb to the middle finger. Continue in this order and restart after you reach the pinky. After eleven minutes, inhale and hold your breath as you twist slowly, moving every muscle in the body. Exhale. Repeat five times. Then sit straight, look at the tip of the nose, and meditate calmly for three minutes.

> MANTRA: *Saa-Taa-Naa-Maa, Raa-Maa-Daa-Saa, Saa-Say-So-Hung*

> TO FINISH: Inhale and hold for thirty seconds while you move the entire body from the head to the toes. Exhale and do that three more times. Inhale and hold the breath, looking at the tip of the nose, for twenty seconds, and then exhale and relax.

To view a video of this, search "ganpati kriya meditation" on YouTube.

The Complete Adi Mantra
for Individual Meditation
11–31 MINUTES

It is said that when this mantra is chanted five times on one breath, the total spiritual knowledge of all teachers who have ever existed or who will ever exist on this earth is accessed. This meditation can help you know what to do in your immediate situation by linking you to your higher consciousness. It can help you handle the stage of spiritual egotism and handle lack of trust in the higher spiritual identity. Do this meditation for a minimum of forty days to achieve the results. You can do it for eleven to thirty-one minutes.

> PREPARATION: Sit tall in a cross-legged position with a slight neck lock. Look at the tip of the nose. Your hands will come together in front of the heart with open palms so your pinkies and side of the hands join. Touch the pointer finger and thumbs together so your hands are in gyan mudra. Your palms are facing up.

> BREATH: Chant the entire mantra 3–5 times on one breath. *Dayv* should be a slightly higher note than the other monotone notes, and *Dayvaa* is slightly drawn out.

> MANTRA: *Ong Namo, Guroo Dayv Namo, Guroo Dayv Namo, Guroo Dayvaa*

> TO FINISH: Relax.

~~~~~~

To view a video of this, search "complete Adi Mantra for individual meditation" on YouTube.

You may have noticed that the kundalini mantras are often spoken very rapidly, and even the rate of many of the exercises is much faster than other types of yoga. The rapid rate of many mantras or movements is all about bringing in maximum prana and conditioning the intercostal muscles to be able to bring in much more oxygen, which is one of the biggest contributors to the benefits of the practice for health and happiness. To newcomers it's whacky, but when you do it, you see why because it changes your mood so you feel so happy. Also, the discipline kundalini yogis develop pours over into other areas of life where they can execute and sustain mentally much more.

White Tantric Yoga

Of all the meditation practices in kundalini yoga, this one is most revered for its powerful ability to enhance happiness and bring you to an altered state long after the meditation. It is a full day of meditation that is only administered by the videos of Yogi Bhajan, who was the living Mahan Tantric before he transitioned out of his body in 2004. The videos work by connecting the students to his subtle body, but also because of the actual structure of the meditation. People are sat in rows across from a partner and knee-to-knee with their neighbor. There is a strong diagonal energy that moves through the lines like a zigzag, which creates a large group aura. There are usually very advanced practitioners in the group who have been meditating daily for twenty or thirty years.

The entire experience will make you feel bright, clear, and positive for about forty days. It is said that one day of this meditation is worth years of meditation on your own. The person who officially facilitates the white tantric program is not the Mahan Tantric, as it was not passed on to someone when Yogi Bhajan transitioned out of his body. The videos are still very powerful guides for the class. There are sometimes hundreds of people at once doing the meditations, which last all day with breaks. In order to prepare for the day, it is best to work on sitting in a meditation position so your hips and knees can handle it, and of course doing kundalini yoga will help you build the stamina. Anyone can attend, and the classes are taught around the world each year. Every-one wears white because it helps expand the electromagnetic field, and they wear a white head covering to help contain the energy and not get a headache. It's best to also bring a white sweater or shawl for relaxation periods as well as a meditation cushion or pad.

White tantric yoga is not to be confused with red or black tantric yoga. It is not sexual, nor does it manipulate others. Red tantric yoga is used for sexual purposes. Black tantra is essentially used to control people, and there are serious negative ramifications for this type of sorcery.

An Inspiring Story

I was always enthralled with the stories my kundalini teachers would tell me about their time working with Yogi Bhajan and the incredible things that would happen. At one point, my teachers found that they needed a bigger house. Houses in Southern California are not cheap. They needed $80,000 for the down payment on a new house and had no idea where it would come from. My teacher started to use the sudarshan chakra kriya, which includes the *Aap Sahaee Hoa* mantra. She said her husband came home and told her that he just made $80,000 and asked her what she did. She smiled. She knew that she had helped manifest the money they needed. It's no wonder she keeps teaching because that's one validation that you won't forget. She had many stories that she would tell us to help us see how these techniques really do work.

I remember each of them because they are so profound. When I was living in a house with young aspiring artists and students, I began to feel like I needed more space to be able to do my morning mantras and meditations without bothering my roommates. We were literally in bunk beds to keep the rent low and allow us the freedom to study. I used the sudarshan chakra kriya, visualizing a place where meditation and yoga were a part of the home. I saw nature and envisioned a white room with sloped ceilings. I immediately found a place with a woman who had an outdoor kitchen and white yurt for rent. She was a yogi and had a meditation room in the house. It was just what I had asked for, but I realized I hadn't asked for a location—and this was thirty miles from work.

I decided to pass and got more specific with the layout of the house. I envisioned a home with a kitchen to the right and stairs on the left. Water was in the back, and my room was upstairs with a sloped ceiling.

There was a stained-glass window on the front door. The first place I looked at was with a retired woman who said basically all she did was go to yoga twice per day and that the room was soundproof, which I liked because I knew I could do morning mantras without bothering her. I moved in and as I was getting things from my car, I turned around and realized I had manifested exactly what was in my vision. There was stained glass right above the front door, the layout was exactly as I pictured, and there was a pool in the back. I began to not be surprised that the meditation worked.

7

Diet, Body Chemistry, and Enlightenment

The role that diet plays in the experience of enlightenment is unquestionable because of so many spiritual traditions that emphasize clean eating in order to harmonize the mind, body, and spirit. Many spiritual systems involve some type of diet recommendation as well as fasting. Now we will focus on how the chemicals in our body affect the kundalini energy so we can activate it. Is there a reason that many cultures eliminate certain meats or all meats from their spiritual systems? It's important to note that many cultures consume meat in a conscious way to avoid it impeding their spiritual progress. We know that Hindus will not eat cow; they consider it sacred. Muslims will not eat pork, many Christian sects will not eat red meat, and some, such as Seventh Day Adventists, eat no meat at all. Some Buddhists, such as the Mahayana, are vegetarian, and kundalini yogis are as well. Some systems make it a point to abstain from alcohol completely, while some use it to enhance spiritual connection. It seems not one spiritual system has ignored the relationship of the soul with what the human consumes. Changing the body's chemistry is something that people have been experimenting with for a long time in order to enhance spiritual awakening of the kundalini energy. After reading about the connection between diet and spiritual awakening such as that practiced by ancient yogis meditating in caves and living on herbs, I altered my diet and found it way easier to connect to psychic abilities.

When we look at the kundalini yoga system, the dietary emphasis can be considered just as important as mantra, breathwork, movement, and meditation. Understanding how certain foods help certain organs and systems allows you to optimize your energy as seasons change. The study of ayurveda, known as the sister science of yoga, is able to help you eat a spiritually enhancing diet that adjusts based on your natural emotional and physical composition as well as the seasons. It is one of the most extensive dietary systems that can help with spiritual attunement and will be explored in detail further in this chapter.

Fasting

Let's take a look into some of the many cultures throughout history that also use fasting as a way to help harmonize the body with the celestial energies. Buddhism, Christianity, Islam, Hinduism, Taoism, and Judaism are just some of the many cultures that incorporate fasting as a spiritual cleansing ritual. If this has been adopted by so many cultures for such a long time, what is it that is happening in the body when we fast that helps us access enlightenment?

Fasting helps in connecting the body to the soul. When you are able to sense from a soul level, you can tune into the all-pervading energy, or unifying field. Fasting helps to cleanse the cells, organs, and tissues of the body while allowing you to cleanse the digestive tract. It also helps you release stored heavy emotional energy, which can make a cleanse a challenge. As you fast, you become more self-aware of how you have used food to pacify your emotions and how you can address them in a healthier way.

Fasting is not something you must do to awaken kundalini, but it does help facilitate it. While I offer this as an optional practice and do have a background in nutrition and wellness, you should always take your own health needs into consideration before deciding to fast.

Fasting Techniques

In kundalini yoga it is recommended not to do a complete fast without first preparing the body gradually. First eliminate toxins such as drugs, alcohol, and processed foods. Eating a light diet of fruits and vegetables is a great way to prepare for a fast. Instead of fasting without any food, you can fast just on vegetables, fruits, and nuts for thirty days. They can be both cooked or uncooked. This diet is said to be rejuvenating. If you do fast without food, you want to break it slowly, as the stomach shrinks and the body becomes more sensitive. Another one of the fasting techniques in kundalini yoga is the rice and mung bean fast, which also includes vegetables, fruit, and chai and is done for thirty days. This is nourishing and helps the organs greatly. Chai tea is a combination of black tea, ginger, cardamom, cloves, black pepper, and cinnamon.

Keep in mind that fasting is not safe for all people due to health concerns, and it's best to consult with your medical provider before starting a fast.

Spiritual Fasting in Different Cultures

BUDDHIST: Buddhist monks do not eat after noon each day until dawn the following day.

CATHOLIC: Ash Wednesday and Good Friday are designated fasting days for Catholics in the US. They also do not eat meat each Friday during Lent.

CHRISTIAN: Christians are encouraged to fast, and believe Jesus's fast for forty days helped his spiritual strength.

HINDU: Ekadashi is a day of fasting twice per month on the eleventh day of the new and full moons. There is fasting at the celebration for Shiva at the beginning of the year and during different days of the week depending on which deities they are working with.

JUDAIC: Yom Kippur is a fasting day each year, and there are at least six other traditional fasting days.

MONGOLIAN SHAMANISM: Shamans would fast for one or two days before going into trance to do spiritual healing.

MUSLIM: Ramadan is observed as a time of fasting each year for thirty days. No food is eaten during daylight hours at that time.

ORTHODOX: There are four major fasting periods in the Orthodox calendar.

PAGAN: Pagans sometimes fast before the spring equinox or as they feel it is needed.

TAOIST: There are usually eight days each month when it is considered best for fasting. *Bigu*, or grain avoidance, is said to help one achieve *xian* (transcendence).

Fasting with Moon Cycles

In the yogic tradition and more specifically in the practice of kundalini yoga, fasting on certain astrological events is a normal practice and has been done for thousands of years.

New Moon

A new moon happens once and sometimes twice each month. This is said to be a time when the veil between worlds is thin and we can tap into spiritual consciousness easier. To enable that, yogis have found it is a good day to fast. One becomes more in tune with their energy and the body can reset its digestive system, giving the major organs a break. Drinking lots of water can help flush the body of toxins to welcome higher spiritual vibrations and emotions that allow us to use this heightened creative energy to grasp the purest ideas that can help the collective.

Full Moon

The healing ring of tantra is done by groups of kundalini yogis on the new moon, eleventh day of the moon, and full moon. Chapter 10 will help explain more how kundalini awakening is linked to astrology in many cultures. The healing ring of tantra is a meditation that must be done very specifically and led by an experienced practitioner. It is beyond the scope of this book but worth mentioning.

Herbs in Different Cultures

Many cultures have discovered different herbs that help awaken the kundalini energy. In South America, one of the most famous and controversial plants, iboga, is known to alter one's consciousness to a state of spiritual transcendence. However, this plant is also something that cannot be taken recreationally because the very ingestion of it is intended to be a sacred, guided quest for spiritual truth. It is one of many plants that are used to grow spiritually. With iboga, there are specific protocols to follow in the way it is prepared and taken as well as what one consumes before taking it. While it may bring you to a state of awakening, it is not something you can go to each day and remain in safely. This is not the only controversial plant known to awaken kundalini energy. Those who study kundalini yoga are adamant that this rapid opening of the kundalini energy is dangerous and that it's safer to gradually awaken it.

Soma, which means drink or liquid, is another controversy. Some researchers of ancient yogic scriptures purport that it is the water element that helps cool and balance the fire element of kundalini, while others claim it points to the ritual of drinking psychedelic plants among the aesthetic yogis before kriya yoga became prevalent.

While this is a whole topic to be studied, that debate is beyond the scope of this book, which is more focused on what everyday people today can do to experience this universal enlightenment of kundalini.

That being said, there is a difference between being high and being in a state of enlightenment. In one you are lucid and able to function, while in the other you are deemed unable to operate a vehicle. However, do not be discouraged about the topic of herbs and their link to kundalini. Similar to the other lifestyle practices, there are herbs that have been found to harmonize the mind and body to help the kundalini awaken. They can be taken in daily dosages, and they do not create severe reactions. One such herb is from Asia and it is called ashitaba. This herb is one of many adaptogenic herbs that help bring the energy of the body into a state of balance. All adaptogens are to be taken on a temporary basis and not long term. However, this herb is touted as the longevity herb for its benefits.

There is a branch of yoga linked to the study of ayurveda called aushadhi, which is the study of herbs and their effect on one's ability to obtain supernatural abilities and awaken kundalini. In Africa, one of the many sacred herbs for divination or accessing spiritual realms is the African dream root, *Silene undulata*, which, similar to the European-derived herb mugwort, induces lucid dreams and heightens intuition. Herbs that help stimulate the pineal gland are not hard to find, and many can be found at local health food stores or online. Most of these herbs are legal and healthy to use daily, whereas other plant extracts such as peyote (of the Native American tradition) and San Pedro (of the South American heritage) have psychoactive effects, causing hallucinations. It is evident that while each Native plant packs a different punch, there are undeniably plants throughout many cultures and time periods that are and have been used to reach enlightenment by awakening kundalini energy.

Explanation of Ayurveda

The system of ayurveda is as vast as the system of yoga. This sister science to yoga covers not just diet but also sleep patterns, personal hygiene practices, and bodily cleansing techniques. The basis of this system pulls from the personality and physical body types that the modern person would recognize as mesomorph, ectomorph, and endomorph. The three types of *doshas* (types) are kapha, pitta, and vatta. Kapha most closely resembles the endomorph. Pitta most closely resembles a mesomorph, and vatta most closely resembles an ectomorph. There are personality traits that fit each kind, and each person is considered to have one that is dominant. They often match physical characteristics exceptionally well, picking up on the link between a person's natural energy levels, metabolism, and emotional states. The goal is to bring harmony and balance in the physical body, energy levels, and personality. Through the use of certain foods, one can create this balance and further their energetic development in yoga.

Raw Food

The practice of eating raw foods to enhance spiritual connection is well documented by yogis. While the practice of living off of herbs in a cave is not as common or practical as it used to be, eating more raw foods can still be done to enhance the flow of energy, build energy, and help activate our kundalini. When we consume raw plants, we are ingesting prana and live cells that actually help detoxify our body and replace our cells. If we have damaged cells straining the body and lowering our energy, raw foods help us rebuild ourselves from the inside out. They help improve our elimination and provide the highest density of nutrients that the body can consume to function optimally.

While some spiritual teachers promote an all raw diet, this can bring the body out of balance energetically in colder seasons because it requires energy to heat up food and digest it. The practice of listening to what your body wants can help you navigate the process of eating raw foods. Raw foods will help you find that foods made by the earth do have good flavor, and over the course of a few weeks of this type of diet, you can retrain your tastebuds to enjoy natural flavor. Raw foods help reduce painful inflammation, brain fog, emotionality caused by low energy and upset stomach, and blood toxicity caused by buildup of waste in the bloodstream that isn't eliminated.

Raw foods have pure energy. Many people are in the habit of blessing their food or praying over their food to amplify the frequency of the food before they consume it. Many people set an intention even for their water, essentially programing the molecules, which have been shown to store energy and be affected by energy. Since water molecules are also in food, praying before a meal might have a bigger effect than we realize. The power of thoughts and words, which are both wavelengths, can help shift energy, and we can help amplify the energy we consume and become with an intention before consumption. We see this similar practice in taking the sacrament of wine and communion wafers as the blood and body of Christ, which is essentially a frequency that spiritual seekers are looking to obtain. It helps us see that this ritual is not about inducing fear of God but likely about helping get in tune with high-vibration consciousness.

Holy water is a tradition in Eastern Orthodox, Catholic, Lutheran, and other religions. Water itself is deeply tied to spiritual awakening as it is used for christenings, baptisms, and the cleansing of one's energy, such as the River Ganga is in India.

The colors of foods are said to help activate the chakras that are linked to the frequency of that color, and overall eating a wide variety of colors can help all the chakras. Chakras are discussed more fully in chapter 8. If you were to practice kundalini yoga and continue to eat processed foods, you may never fully realize the benefits nor have your kundalini rise. Just to clarify, raw foods do not include animal products such as raw fish or raw dairy.

Certain foods that help decalcify the pineal gland include garlic, oregano oil, lemons, and goji berries. The more raw foods you eat, the faster your pineal gland can start to function. Removing fluoride is essential to decalcifying it as well. Fluoride is in most tap waters and even many bottled waters. You can get fluoride-free toothpaste and artesian well water to work on getting this gland active again.

Alkalinity

Because the body conducts energy, we are like a battery. The more alkaline we are, the more energy we can hold. The modern-day diet of fast food and beer acidifies the body, blocking the ability to increase the energy level in the body. Most cooked grain-based foods are acidifying. Pizza, pasta, desserts, bagels, meat, caffeine, alcohol, sugar, chips, and candy are all examples of acidic foods.

Plants are naturally alkaline and will help you be able to handle more energy. They help reduce acid that causes ulcers and acid reflux and lower inflammation caused by acidic hormones like cortisol. Alkalizing your body is easy if you eat green smoothies, salads, steamed vegetables, herbal teas, and alkaline water. It will make a big difference in your spiritual progress from a purely physical function standpoint.

Drug Chemistry Compared to Kundalini Yoga

In Yogi Bhajan's book *Kundalini Yoga: The Flow of Eternal Power,* he said, "If you have to be addicted to something, be addicted to doing sadhana daily. Otherwise, addiction is not a source of freedom."

Why not just use drugs to achieve a state of enlightenment? Many people do. What is often achieved through altered states can also be achieved with kundalini yoga but in a more controlled and safe way. To understand our true identity in a spiritual sense, it's important to know what is happening in the body when we reach altered states of consciousness. Drugs have caused statistically significant levels of pain and loss of life, while kundalini yoga can offer this elated state without the harmful dangers of drugs.

A psychonaut is someone who studies altered states of consciousness, and psychonautics is the methodology for explaining altered states of consciousness. Psychonauts use different means by which to study altered states of consciousness, including sensory deprivation, lucid dreaming, hallucinogens, and brainwave entrainment. The use of entheogens for spiritual and creative enhancement is the study of some psychonauts. While some psychonauts are able to tolerate high levels of LSD or other substances, not all bodies respond the same to these substances. Although this chapter doesn't cover it, the study of psychonautic entheogens is a big part of the spiritual community, and you can find intellectual material regarding the expansion of consciousness from the experience of these experts. This chapter helps us understand how most people experience these substances without having the rare ability to tolerate them as a psychonaut expert does under observed and controlled environments. This is to better understand the states that one can reach using drugs and compare them to kundalini yoga to see if there is a benefit to one or the other.

Prevalence of Addiction Across Cultures

Drug use is going up, and treatment is not readily available. People are seeking the release they feel from drugs whether they are seeking relief from physical or emotional pain. The UN's 2019 World Drug Report reveals the use of opioids increased by 56 percent from 2016 to 2017. The staggering truth is in 2017, 53.4 million people used opioids. The production of cocaine increased by 25 percent in 2017, and more cocaine was seized in 2017 than any other year. Only one in seven people globally are being treated for drug addiction, and the numbers of addictions are skyrocketing. More than 47,000 opioid deaths were reported in North America in 2017, which was a 13 percent increase from 2016. The American Medical Association reported that more than forty states saw an increase in opiod-linked deaths in 2020, and the CDC reported 13 percent of Americans increased substance abuse due to COVID-19 (Abramson 2021). In November 2021 many news sources released staggering reports backed by the CDC of over 100,000 drug overdoses in one year, which is a record high.

In a country where treatment programs are available, the numbers are still rising. In other countries where there are far less treatment programs, addiction is even more of a threat. There are new synthetic drugs that continue to enter the market globally, and just a quick glance at some of these statistics is a sobering and cold truth. Drugs are causing serious problems. While there are clinical applications of certain drugs for trauma therapy, the careful monitoring is not happening for those losing their lives, destroying their families, and destabilizing communities.

As you read through the following destructive properties of the substances people sometimes use to try to enhance meditation, you'll notice the benefits they offer are also available through kundalini yoga without the negative effects. The body naturally produces painkillers, serotonin, and dopamine, and it can produce its own energy and alertness if one knows how to do it. However, trying to use a pill (without doctor supervision) or substance uncategorically causes more harm than good. When you're looking for a biohack or a brainhack, look to a safer solution: kundalini yoga. What person can afford to be out of control of their body, unable to use their memory, or in a state of grandiosity or psychosis? Drugs are not a sustainable, safe solution to our quest to feel better or euphoric. We need to change the program.

ACID (ALSO KNOWN AS LSD): This substance changes the serotonin levels in the brain. It also increases electrical activity and blood flow to the brain. It can make people feel relaxed and happy, but there's no guarantee that you won't get a bad trip and feel paranoid and scared. It can also cause flashbacks as well as permanently damage the brain. It often makes people completely out of control of their body, unable to function for about fifteen hours. It can cause hallucinations, palpitations, anxiety, trauma from a bad trip, and persistent psychosis, where one is unable to think clearly, has a distorted sense of time, and long-term cannot communicate with others or think rationally.

DMT: This increases serotonin levels in the brain and affects the way the brain perceives visual and auditory information. It causes hallucinations and sometimes mystical experiences. It can cause loss of muscle coordination and chest pain, as well as permanent damage to mental and physical health. This is the active ingredient in ayahuasca, which has been

used in spiritual healing ceremonies for thousands of
years. It is naturally produced by the body, but taking it
recreationally introduces a much higher dosage.

MARIJUANA: Long-term use of this plant has been found
to create permanent adverse changes in the brain such as
cognitive and memory impairment. This can worsen the
symptoms of depression, create panic and anxiety, and be
addictive. It can leave you unable to function for hours at
a time and can create a dependency because it creates an
abundance of dopamine and a sense of euphoria. It can
worsen mental health conditions as well.

MUSHROOMS: The psychoactive form of mushrooms causes
hallucinations. They can cause anxiety during a trip. They
are also sometimes known to cause recurring hallucinations
afterward. They distort our sense of time and can sometimes
provide a sense of relaxation. They create more activity in
the brain where there is usually not crosstalk, neurologically
speaking.

An Inspiring Story

When I was living in Los Angeles, I had the opportunity to get to
know devout kundalini yogis who swore by the benefits of kundalini
yoga. One was a kundalini teacher who was certainly hooked to the
euphoria it provided. He had been a drug dealer in college and ended
up going to jail for it. He found kundalini yoga and never looked back.
One thing I'll never forget is how he always said, "I am trying to get
high and stay high." Instead of spending tons of money trying to get
high and getting in all sorts of legal trouble, as a kundalini yoga teacher
he was able to make money teaching and helping people develop tools
to elevate their mind, body, and spirit. He had a glowing and quirky
energy that made it seem as if he knew the secret elixir to life. His skin
was clear, and he could function on very little sleep. He wasn't the only
kundalini yogi I knew that was more productive than other people on

less sleep; most of the teachers I knew needed very little sleep because of the extra energy they held in their nervous system.

Another inspiring story I came across was a teacher who had lived a life of privilege. He was given money and didn't have responsibility. This had led him to drink, do drugs, and almost die. He found kundalini yoga, recovered from his addictions, and found that he enjoyed being a yogi and helping others much more. The benefits he felt from kundalini yoga made it so he never felt the need to pick up drugs again. Stories like these were very common, and I met many more people who used kundalini yoga to recover from drug addiction.

While drug addiction is not something that every person deals with, something that many of us do face in this day and age is the temptation to drink heavily because it is so normalized in our culture. A good friend of mine who is also a teacher found herself in a dark place just being a part of everyday society. Alcohol abuse wasn't something she could function with, and it led her to find kundalini yoga. Her happiness went up, and her inspiration to help others find the stability and tools to feel happy without substances is very strong. She continues to teach and lead retreats to help people find something they didn't know existed as an alternative approach to finding happiness and living in control of your emotions.

A Diet-Related Inspiring Story

I had eaten raw for about eight months straight when I had my first spiritual awakening that was noticeable. I was seeing synchronicities all the time, having premonitions, and was able to reach other realms in dreams and meditation. I had stopped drinking alcohol as well. The body was responding to the diet as my energy shifted. The first thing I realized was how much food is directly linked to emotions. I found the better I ate, the easier it was for me to have positive emotions. The next thing I realized was how the vibration of the food I consumed allowed me to perceive the actual group consciousness thought forms that mostly run society. I could basically read the energy of groups and also just predict someone's behavior and mindset very quickly. I could sense things at a distance and was able to use energy to manifest, heal, and move energy. The cravings for processed foods also went away.

As you detox your body, your mind also detoxes. I found a direct correlation between who I allowed in my life and the type of people I attracted by eating clean foods. It also enhances psychic abilities significantly. I could pretty much guess what a person was eating based on the energy they had. When we are trying to break deeply ingrained habits of fear-based thinking, addiction to egoic thought patterns, and feeling the need to fit in with social circles that are not going to support our soul's growth, our food is as much our secret weapon as our breathwork, meditation, and movement practice.

I feel raw foods gave me a direct ticket to higher states of consciousness. Eating mostly salads and smoothies helped me stay feeling positive and clear to be able to offer many healings and readings for clients. I felt that it was a part of the job to eat that way and knew that if I was eating heavier, more dense food, I would have a much harder time doing the healing work. Books about spiritual nutrition helped inspire me to think of my body in an energetic sense and to cleanse it in order to access the kundalini energy. This is a major part of how I started to unlock the energy that is available in my body and be able to store more of it. I became alkalized for the first time in my life and stopped going through spells of hunger, bloating, and fatigue that I had experienced my whole life from eating cooked foods and grains. I was able to shed the old behaviors that I thought were "me" and that I thought I had no other choice but to live with.

Toxic behavior patterns in my life were greatly eliminated by simply changing my diet. I'll back up a little more to explain how much changing my diet freed me from a painful, joyless life. How all this started was through my diet. I felt as if I was dragging myself through the day, living in jail but not locked up. I had no energy, no motivation to work out, and couldn't find an ounce of happiness. It was brutal. I started having a raw smoothie with superfoods each morning, and my energy started to shift. I started feeling more compassion for myself and started to get a glimpse of a truth that helped me come back to life. I began to feel hopeful again. This was the beginning of reclaiming my power and finding a solution to my unhappiness. It was a first step in re-creating myself and breaking away from mainstream society, where my ego was in charge of my decision making. Changing my diet helped me break away from a toxic job and toxic group of friends. It helped me find yoga and a career and a group of friends where I feel safe and cared for.

*Those people who have a very strong
magnetic field—electric charge,
life force, circumvent force—can
liberate others with touch and
mental projection, and where their
steps shall be, there truth shall be.*

Yogi Bhajan

8

Chakra Work

In the quest of reaching enlightenment, it is essential to work on each of your energy centers—your chakras—to allow the kundalini energy to flow. Doing chakra healing work in addition to a kundalini yoga and meditation practice allows you to fine-tune your personal energy, raise your frequency, and access higher states of consciousness.

There are time-tested tools and techniques to target each chakra that work with the elements of nature and incorporate traditional hatha yoga. Crystals and essential oils are high-vibrational natural items that interact with your own energy. Understanding how to use them to heal a specific chakra can help you in your quest to understand yourself on an energetic and spiritual level.

Crystals

Another phenomenon that has been sacred in many cultures for the spiritual value and accessibility it offers is the use of crystals to reach transcended states of consciousness, which essentially provide the experience of enlightenment. As vibratory tools, crystals help activate the chakras; these effects have been reported in cultures that are completely separate from each other, with similar reports on similar varieties having unique effects. Often the colors of the crystals match the color of the chakra that it helps heal.

Certain crystals are also known to help with healing specific emotional issues, which we can correlate to the chakra most closely linked to those emotions. As the emotional component is intricately tied to the physical component, we know that both must be optimized to allow the kundalini to raise to the head. Crystals help raise the kundalini, and there are absolutely some that pack a bigger punch than others. Some people who have already become very sensitive to energy can sense electricity within the crystal or subtle vibrations within themselves that show them where the crystal resonates. The study of crystals and their properties is already widely known, so for the purposes of this book, we will merely list some that have the highest frequency to save you the trouble of purchasing thousands of crystals until you finally find the ones that have this very high frequency that will shift your energy quickly.

Crystals known to awaken kundalini directly include moldavite, phenacite, and apophyllite. Moldavite increases your energy, and people say they can't sleep while wearing it; if they wear it while exercising, they have too much energy. Phenacite and apophyllite have both been said to be some of the highest-vibration crystals, and apophyllite specifically is widely regarded as the best crystal for kundalini awakening.

Poses

Certain yoga poses target certain areas that are linked to the chakras. If you are dealing with stiffness in an area of the body, it could have an energetic root that can be worked on with breathing and poses that target that area. It's important to be flexible enough to be able to sit comfortably in meditation for at least thirty minutes. Similarly, you'll need a flexible spine and strong core. If you're starting out without the muscles that will help you in meditation, you can do extra poses in addition to kriyas to help bring balance into your body. We think of the body in terms of right and left needing to be in balance, the front and back needing to be in balance, and the strength and flexibility needing to be in balance. When any of these foundations are out of balance, it's hard to reach alignment.

Getting to know the body better will help you tune into your body to see where you can improve. Often fatigue in meditation comes from tightness in the shoulders and compression in the lower back, which is leaking our energy. These poses are from hatha yoga and are to be done with slow ujjayi breathing, as described in the chapter on breathwork. Be sure to work on this breathing technique before going into the pose, and make sure you focus on doing it the whole time or you will forfeit the full spectrum of benefits physically and energetically. If you find you get out of breath doing kriyas, hatha yoga can help build some core breath endurance; however, the high levels of oxygen in both will build muscle and breath endurance quickly if you really make the breathing a powerful part.

Getting your head below your heart in some of these poses helps reverse circulation to send blood and prana to the upper chakras and stimulate them, which induces more positive emotions and consequently helps raise your frequency.

Chair Pose

Chair pose helps build core stability and improves postural alignment. It will help you build the strength to do more physically challenging standing poses and helps your root chakra as you create stability in your foot and ankle muscles. Stand with your feet hip-distance apart and sit back as if you're going to sit into a chair. Raise the arms straight up in line with your ears with your palms facing. Activate your feet and continue to raise the chest without flaying the ribs out. Hold the pose as you breathe deeply for five rounds of ujjayi breathing.

Horse Pose

Common in martial arts training, this pose helps align the spine and build endurance and strength while stretching the hips. It helps you strengthen your core and improves or corrects posture. It helps to activate the sacral chakra energy. Take a wide stance and squat so your hips are at the level of your knees. Keep your torso tall and tuck the tailbone as you knit your front ribs in. Keep the shoulder blades down the back. Bring your arms to the sides with elbows touching the ribs and your hands in gyan mudra placing the thumb and pointer finger together. Alternatively, bring palms together in prayer pose in front of your chest. Hold the pose for five slow, deep rounds of ujjayi breathing.

Camel Pose

This pose can help correct the hunched position caused by working on computers or looking at cell phones. It helps activate the solar plexus, heart, and throat chakras. It will increase your energy levels and help improve spinal flexibility.

Stand on your knees with the knees hip-distance apart. Think of lifting up and out of your lower back. Place your hands on your lower back with your fingers pointing down. Lift the chest up and back like a waterfall and look up and back but keep a slight tuck to the chin. Keep the lower abdomen engaged to protect the lower back, and only go as far as is comfortable. Do not hold your breath. If it's accessible, reach one hand and then the other to the heels with straight arms.

Hold the pose for five slow, deep breaths. To come out of the pose, place hands on your lower back to help yourself come back to neutral. Repeat a few times. It's helpful to do pelvic tucks after backbends to neutralize the spine.

Wheel Pose

This helps open all of the chakras and is very energizing. If you want to create strength and flexibility, this will challenge both. If you have tight shoulders, quads, or hip flexors, this will be a good gauge to help you see what you really need to work on. It will help your whole body move easier once you're able to do it, as it greatly increases spinal flexibility. Work up to it slowly, and stop if there is pain in the lower back.

Lie on your back and bend your knees, placing your feet flat on the floor hip-distance apart. Place your palms down next to your ears with fingertips pointing toward your shoulders. Press into your feet and hands and lift your body to first rest on your head. Bring your elbows in so they are in line with your shoulders and then press again, working on

136

straightening your legs and arms, which takes lots of practice. Take five slow, deep breaths and then slowly lower down. Repeat a few times and then hug knees to your chest gently to neutralize the spine.

Plow Pose

This is considered the queen of all hatha yoga poses. It stretches the life nerve, which runs along the back side of the body. It will help digestion, speed up your metabolism, release blocks, and improve thyroid function. Eventually you'll be able to stay in it for a few minutes and feel clear-headed and energized afterward. It specifically helps your throat chakra. Lie on your back and lift your legs as if you're going to stand on the ceiling. Do not look side to side in this pose to protect the smaller vertebrae in the upper spine and neck. Lift your hips up so your feet go over your head and toes come to the ground. Try to keep the spine straight up and down so your chest comes to your chin. Don't let the spine curve. If possible, scoot your shoulder blades together and interlace your hands with straight arms. Take five slow, deep breaths, then unlace your hands and slowly bring your spine back to the ground one vertebra at a time.

Intuition Tools

Yogis call their practice a lifestyle because there are so many little actions throughout the day that help them stay in a high state of emotional resonance. Their intuition-enhancing tools are used globally, and the benefits are easy to experience. Some of the practices are not as well-known, and some common ones are not usually understood fully for the energetic aid they provide. You'll see that yogis incorporate many items of nature into their life to help stay in tune with universal energy. These tools include the elements of fire, air, water, and earth.

Essential Oils and Incense

When we create a sacred space, our body becomes used to going into a deep state of meditation there. The space holds the energetic vibration and helps us go into deeper brain wave states more quickly. Using the same scents can help your brain be triggered into a meditative state as well. The sense of smell is able to quickly trigger the memory. Essential oils and incense will also help raise the vibration of the space by clearing and purifying the air of energy-depleting positive ions produced by electronics. Essential oils and incense can also help clear your chakras. Certain oils and smells are known to help with different aspects of emotional healing, which have a direct effect on your chakras. You can always burn incense if you feel the energy needs sprucing up after someone negative has been there or if you felt your own energy left an imprint.

Frankincense was one of the gifts said to have been given to baby Jesus. It is also one of the things tomb raiders sought when raiding. Its high vibration helps one access the spiritual realm by stimulating the upper chakras.

Meditation Beads

Beads are known as power objects in many cultures, and the actual bead itself is known to have certain properties that can help and enhance your chakras based on what it is made out of. Beads made from crystals correspond to the chakras that match their frequency on the visible light spectrum (color). Woods from different trees and seeds also have subtle resonance as scents that can help induce a state of meditation. The number of recitations, which is usually 108, is done to create a consistent energetic projection, and the care of the beads can help them become a charged object that holds a frequency of healing because of your intention.

If you used a set of beads to focus on raising your kundalini energy, the energy from meditation and mantra recitation could then be worn with you throughout the day to carry the energy and remind you of your intention. You can find mantras to recite online or use my book *Modern Guide to Meditation Beads*. The actual structure of the necklace is said to represent or symbolize the awakening, with the beads joined by a knot and a guru bead and tassel as if the bead was the third eye and the tassel was energy expanding up from the crown chakra.

Gongs

The gong is a sacred tool to be used only with proper training. It can help clear the subconscious mind just as a massage helps clear tension in the body. When played by a trained yogi who is focused on a mantra, the gong amplifies the yogi's intention, which beams energy into the room and interacts with the subtle body and energetic system. This allows for deep relaxation, and one can sense energetic blocks essentially being released as the sound moves through the energy and raises the vibration. It is deeply healing, and it is strongly advised that you only listen to gongs played by a trained kundalini yoga teacher that you personally trust, as someone without a clear intention could essentially be amplifying negative energy.

Natural Fibers

This helps collect your meditative energy day after day. Natural fibers hold a resonance, and using the same meditation mat of wool or organic cotton as well as a natural fiber meditation shawl are ways to help induce a deeper meditative state more quickly. Wool, cotton, silk, and hemp are all able to help with meditation when used repeatedly.

Attire

Wearing light-colored loose clothing can help expand your aura and allow you to enter a deeper, more meditative state. Kundalini yogis wear modest clothing to keep the focus from being on the physical and allow us to concentrate deeper in meditation without the usual popularity contest so common in our culture.

Playing Mantras in Your Space

This will affect the water in your body by helping all the molecules feel peaceful and harmonized. We are about 75 percent water and the energy we are in or exposed to affects the energy in our body. Playing mantras on a low volume as you sleep helps stop nightmares and keeps you from generating stress hormones while you sleep. It also helps you so that when you wake up, your aura is not full of negative molecules of emotion (electromagnetic energy that feels heavy). It gives you an advantage in your energetic work.

You can purchase meditation mantra tracks or find them for free on YouTube. You may choose to record them in your own voice and play them that way.

Meditation Cushions

One difference you'll see in a meditation class is there are meditation cushions to sit on. There is actually a technical reason for this. For some of us who have tight hips and IT bands, sitting cross-legged on the floor means that our knees are above our hips and blood cannot flow to the feet. Ideally, we have the knees below the hips and sit on the edge of the meditation cushion to help reduce the tendency for the spine to hunch. When the pelvis is tilted forward slightly, instead of backward (if you think of it like a bowl), it helps us keep the spine upright and reduces lower back pain that can cause distraction. Putting the tops of the feet on the ground with the heels up at the perineum can help create a sense of stability in the body at the base of the spine. Sometimes a cushion isn't quite enough support, and a small wooden meditation bench with a slight angle is used so the knees can be on the ground without too much pressure on them or the ankles. The whole goal is to keep the spine straight, reduce pain in the body, and allow as little distractions as possible for meditation.

An Inspiring Story

I doubted that healing energy could be passed from one person to another until I decided to become Reiki certified for my thirtieth birthday. I was surprised that my hands felt a buzzing energy as I learned to work with the energy. I also found that I could feel where people were working on me even when their hands were not touching me. I noticed people's muscles would twitch when I would hold my hands over their muscles even without touching them and without them seeing where my hands were. The subtle pressure, heat, and tingling felt during a Reiki session helped me really develop a working relationship with the chakras. Let me back up a bit here. When I first started giving readings in Orange County, I was using what people call clairsentience. I would essentially get most of my information about another person through the chakras. I would feel what they were feeling and go from there based on what that chakra related to. It was accurate but tiring because I ended up feeling any number of things on a shift.

Doing healing work and Reiki still allowed me to read someone's chakras, but I could also move energy to help release a blocked chakra. It was still hard work, though. Often, I would feel a client's physical symptoms a day before they booked with me and before I met them. One time I had sudden shoulder pain for a day, and when a client came in who had just been in a car accident, it was the same shoulder that had been hurting on me, and the pain went away when I asked them about it. Other clients have come in and I've gotten their headaches and called them out for not drinking enough water. Some have had bad anxiety that I picked up on ahead of time as well. This energetic communication is something that I could pick up on pretty easily as I became more tuned into energy.

One time a client came in for a Reiki session and my process was to work on each chakra until they all felt like they were flowing. In this session, she was on her stomach, and I had my hands over her back where her heart chakra is located. I got a gripping pain in my chest and psychically observed negative energy flying out from her back and away from her. As we chatted after the session, I asked if she had any heart problems. She said no but that her chest had hurt when she was lying on her stomach just then. We had both simultaneously experienced her energy healing where I was using the technique to add healing energy and the intention to help her heal.

We are not fools when we tell you, "Get up in the morning and have a cold shower."

Yogi Bhajan

9

Cold Water Therapy

Cold water showers are one of the key components in the practice of kundalini yoga. They are used to help detoxify the body and create a strong nervous system. Both of those things are key to being able to raise your frequency to activate the upper chakras and allow your kundalini to rise.

Cold showers are not new as a healing and spiritual modality. The practice of using hydrotherapy is traced all the way back to the ancient civilizations in Greece, China, Rome, and Egypt. Using the cold as a medical cure is mentioned in texts dating back to 1600 BCE. The yogis' use of *ishnaan* also dates way back. Ishnaan is essentially the body being able to maintain its temperature despite the cold. It also has what the yogis call the ability to make someone ageless. Yogi Bhajan said his teacher did not age because of cold water therapy. He also stressed that there are more intricacies involved in how to take a cold shower.

Mark Twain spoke of the cold water cure. Hippocrates, the founder of modern medicine, promoted hydrotherapy. Benedictine monks also promoted hydrotherapy, and the uses of it have been shown to be both for physical and spiritual healing. Swamis, Tibetan monks, and yogis in the Himalayas are known to meditate in the winter with barely anything on. They are able to melt the snow around them.

Today, many people do ice plunges, filling their tub with ice water or jump in cold ocean, lake, or pool water as another form of hydrotherapy. Kundalini yogis have an intricate process for cold water showers that takes about 12–15 minutes.

Immune System Benefits

The body becomes more able to handle stress and the cells are rejuvenated. When the cold water hits the skin, the blood rushes to the skin. The blood will rush back to the organs and flush them when you step out of the cold water. This is said to help the glands secrete to boost health and vitality and stop the cells in the body from aging. This is why there is a system in kundalini yoga of getting in and out of the cold water three or four times in one shower. The cold water is not supposed to run directly on the thighs, and menstruating or pregnant women should take lukewarm showers. If you have heart disease, a fever, or rheumatism, do not take cold showers. If you have high blood pressure, move slowly.

When you take the cold water shower, the capillaries in your organs open up, allowing fresh new blood to enter them and nourish them with oxygen. Cold water can be used at different points on your body to stimulate different effects. For example, you can run the bottoms of your feet under cold water to stimulate the 72,000 nerve endings there and give yourself a second wind.

Ultimately having strong immunity and nerves helps you feel good, which boosts your mood and helps you have a strong daily yoga practice. It also helps you have the energy to practice!

Dry Brushing

Before they get in the shower, kundalini yogis begin with a simple dry brushing of the body to remove dead skin cells. A soft brush will help prepare the body's outer layer. You don't want to use hard bristles that scrape the skin. You can find a natural bristle dry skin brush in the bath section of a natural foods store. Sometimes they are called spa brushes, and they often have a wood base with a strap handle for your hand.

Brush with long strokes, starting with the hands and feet and moving toward your heart. This is the traditional direction that dry brushing is done in. It will leave your skin feeling soft, and it is best to do this in the morning before your shower.

Almond Oil

The more extensive type of cold water therapy practiced in kundalini yoga also involves almond oil. The body is rubbed with pure almond oil after dry brushing and before getting into the cold shower. This can help brace the body against the water, adding another layer. Using this type of oil specifically ensures you will not be greasy after your shower, and it has many minerals that improve your skin health.

How to Take a Cold Shower

Some kundalini yogis prefer to wear loose cotton shorts to protect the thighs from cold water. The thigh area is said to control the calcium-magnesium balance, and the femur bone is not to be exposed to cold water. Once you're in the water, massaging the body helps to stimulate blood flow. You can chant a mantra while you're taking your cold shower as well. To massage, start with the hands and feet and move inward. They also use their feet to massage their lower legs and opposite feet. Do not stay under the cold water long. Take a break and turn off the shower a few times. When you turn off the shower, continue to massage. Massage the breasts to help expel toxins. After a few rounds of this, which will take about ten minutes, you will find you are warm. Running the water directly on the forehead helps you feel clear headed.

When you rub your hands together, you create heat. When you massage your body, you will heat up your body under the cold water. The yogis turn the shower on and off about three times, massaging each time. After the shower, wrap in a big warm towel to let the skin heat up; the blood will go back to the organs to flush them. The entire body is nourished with this process and the body can fight off cold. It is said that this is more effective on the cells than practicing yoga for hours. It is an ancient process that helps to rebuild organ health.

This bath is for your circulation and nerves and is not considered bathing. You can wash your hair and body in a separate shower at night with warm water.

An Inspiring Story

A teacher I know in Los Angeles always started his kundalini classes talking about the life-transforming power of cold showers, which always seemed a funny choice to me. I didn't quite understand the real benefits of cold water therapy and why he always talked about cold showers habitually at the beginning of his classes. This teacher was one of the most disciplined, consistent, and dedicated teachers I knew, and over time, I realized it was likely that I was underestimating the benefits of this part of the practice that he so adamantly praised.

I didn't want to feel cold and I didn't want to forgo my nice warm shower. However, once I took the kundalini teacher training and learned about what happens in your body when you do this, I realized how beneficial it really was. I can now see how the showers helped me have strong creativity, high energy, and clear focus. The focus and ability to block out distractions from mainstream society were very apparent with this teacher as well. His progress as a leader was remarkable. He taught all around the world, maintained his daily practice, and never seemed to be in a bad mood. Perhaps his secret tip at the beginning of class was not because he didn't understand kundalini yoga well enough to offer some profound insights into the nature of existence but because he had found a biohack that worked quickly and effectively and genuinely wanted people to do it too.

10

Following Astrology

Within the many cultures who have discovered the kundalini energy, there is an inextricable link to planetary energies. Even Easter and other common Western holidays correspond to the energy that is activated within us from the planets on certain days where planets align each season. In fact, most of our major holidays in the West have astrological origins. We discussed how yogis have used the moon to time their fasting as a part of the lifestyle of awakening kundalini. Now we are going to look at how to move with the energy of the universe to understand the vibratory effect the planets have on our own psyche, emotions, and energy levels.

When you're working diligently toward the ultimate goal of enlightenment, there are going to be days when you have lots of energy and days when you have much less. Understanding and tracking the planetary movements improves your intuition and wisdom to be able to move with the tides that are running through all of humanity and use your energy wisely. Moving your own energy to the state of enlightenment could be a lifelong journey or it could happen quickly. You may reach it and then work to get back there. To maintain it, knowing the energy of each day and how the cycles affect people will help you see the fabric of reality as something that makes more sense and is less chaotic. Just as we started to understand how people have visions with rainbow colors when their third eye opens by understanding a law of thermodynamics, we can use this ancient system to also see into our own soul as well as better understand others.

The universal experience of enlightenment is not just about escaping everyday life; in the practice of kundalini yoga, it's about being able to maneuver in it with much more skill and intelligence. Energy intelligence is no longer reserved for the rishis, the saints, or the mages. As we evolve as a species, it is something that is being more readily understood and realized. Part of the lifestyle of living energetically intelligent, just as we know we should sleep with the cycle of night and day, is knowing the larger cycles with which we can heal certain parts of our own energy to continue our spiritual path toward superconsciousness.

Feeling confused? Keep reading, and it will start to make more sense.

Astrology in Different Cultures

First of all, let's look at how astrology has been linked to the universal experience of enlightenment in many times and places, and then we will start to see how this is tied into kundalini. There are entirely unique systems of astrology in China, India, Ireland, Native American cultures, South America, and Africa. Most of us probably think astrology came from Egypt because there are more popularized stories of the pharaohs relying on their astrologers; however, looking deep into ancient civilizations across the world, we find astrology was practiced universally as a map to the soul and the unification of consciousness.

The Chinese zodiac includes twelve animals. The day is divided into two-hour segments that are each linked to one of the animals.

This expands deeper into the meridian clock, which shows the yin and yang changing every two hours and indicates how the body's organs are affected by this constant ebb and flow of energy. Northern Mongolian shamans were known to do their spirit walking between the physical and spiritual world during the horse hour, from 11 AM to 1 PM, when it was easier for them to enter a trancelike state. They are then able to predict the future and see energetic dimensions to bring through healing for people. This zodiac clock can be expanded over larger periods of time and is a twelve-year cycle as well.

In India, the ayurvedic clock is similar in that specific times of the day are considered best for doing certain things based on the energy that is available. Certain times such as 10 AM to 2 PM are filled with energy, while others are best for resting. This system is designed to help restore the balance of your energy by getting you in tune with nature's cycle and the energy of the earth. It also is directly linked to the body and helps one maintain optimal energy through its practices. The kundalini yoga practice of meditating before the sun rises to enhance spiritual connection is also based on the angle of the sun to the earth at that time. The yogic practice of meditating at both twilight times for enhanced spiritual connection is a practice reflected in other cultures as well. Many cultures have adopted the practice of morning prayers to enhance one's connection to an awakened state of spiritual consciousness.

We can trace our Western astrology to ancient Rome, which adapted it from the Greeks, who adapted it from the Babylonians from Mesopotamia. The Sumerians of Mesopotamia are said to have given the world astrology and have the first record of it. The Roman gods that went on to influence Paganism were then assimilated into modern-day Christianity, as many of their festivals became our current religious holidays. The stories of the gods that come from polytheistic religions seeded the soil for monotheism, although this is not promoted by leaders of monotheism. This book, however, is not to debunk religious systems but to show how all spiritual systems have common threads about the experience and path to enlightenment based upon common lifestyle practices that raise kundalini. The specific verbiage, theologians report, is a projection of the time, based on how the society leaders felt they needed to construct order and peace. The goal of this book is to adapt to where we are now and use the historic practices of reaching the experience of enlightenment that are common throughout time and culture.

So just how can we make sense of so many different systems with different gods and zodiac signs that all claim to bring us closer to a state of enlightened consciousness? We will look at some easy yogic practices that help us align our energy. Knowing when to do what type of energetic healing in the yogic system helps a practitioner choose which type of activity to do and which energy center to focus on. This bypasses the need to induce a trancelike state through some more crude means some healers have developed, such as asphyxiation. While this might not kick down the door to enlightenment instantly, with measured efforts working with the cycles of nature and the planets can get you there safely. You can still work your day job and stay in tune with planetary movements. The more you know the energies of the sky, the easier it is to tune into your energy and balance it to harmonize it and allow higher vibrational frequencies to enter the mind space.

Planets and Chakras

Yogis and pagans both found that the body was prime for certain spiritual and energetic work on certain days. While the yogis focus on specific chakras that correlate to specific astrological placements, the pagans found that certain herbs were best used for spiritual ritual and purposes on certain days. The web of connected energy between our own bodies is seen to be connected to the celestial bodies in many cultures. Doing certain kundalini awakening rituals based around the movement of the planets dates back to pre-Christian times.

Days of the Week and Planets

Each day of the week is associated with a classical planet and body part. As yoga teachers plan their daily vinyasa or hatha classes, they often pick up on what the collective needs on each day, and the joke among yoga teachers is that they all communicated before planning their classes because so often they focus on the same body parts as other teachers on the same days. While this is not just based on the planet that rules each day of the week, it is because yoga teachers are tapping into the frequency of compassion to ask what is best for healing on that day, and the many layers of planetary influences can help them find that focus for their class. Kundalini yoga teachers often intentionally plan their classes based on a special planetary event. If you're practicing at home, you can choose meditations that target certain body parts or emotional aspects based on the day of the week to practice efficiently. Just as there are seven days of the week, there are seven chakras in the body.

> MONDAY is ruled by the Moon. This planet is linked to the heart chakra. This is a good day to work on healing and grief. The Moon influences our emotions, our intuition, and our spiritual connection.

> TUESDAY is ruled by Mars. This planet is linked to the root chakra. This is a good day to work on stability and vitality or overcoming fears. Mars influences our passion, motivation, and energy.

> WEDNESDAY is ruled by Mercury. This planet is linked to the throat chakra. This is a good day to work on expression and communication. Mercury influences electronics, the mail, travel, and speaking.

> THURSDAY is ruled by Jupiter. This planet is linked to the crown chakra. This is a good day to work on abundance and soul connection. Jupiter influences expansion, luck, and fortune.

FRIDAY is ruled by Venus. This planet is linked to the sacral chakra. This is a good day to work on healing addiction, manifesting, and activating creativity. Venus influences art, love, romance, and beauty.

SATURDAY is ruled by Saturn. This planet is linked to the third eye chakra. This is a good day to work on karma and intuition. Saturn has to do with time, learning lessons, responsibility, limitations, and institutions.

SUNDAY is ruled by the Sun. This planet is linked to the solar plexus chakra. This is a good day to work on awakening your personal power and removing negativity. The Sun influences our willpower, leadership abilities, confidence, joy, charisma, and optimism.

The other planets that don't govern days of the week will still be important to know when using astrology to help in the process of awakening. Uranus is the planet of rebellion and independence. Pluto is the planet that influences the subconscious and our shadow aspects. Neptune is the planet that influences our dreams and imagination. As these planets move through the sky, we will better understand the layers of energy we are experiencing.

Signs

While there are different signs and symbols in different cultures, they share many common traits. You may find that your Chinese zodiac year animal and element often describes similar traits in your Western astrology birth chart. To understand yourself and heal your own energy, it's important in many cultures to honor the position of the celestial bodies at the time of birth. Since enlightenment is about tapping into the energy that connects all things, to access a true sense of enlightenment we must also look at our current soul energy imprint on the energetic whole to bring our energy into harmony and generate more positive energy. We must start in the dirt to grow into the lotus. Our mind and ego personality must be understood so it does not stand in the way of our spiritual progress. The trifecta of mind, body, and soul are all equally important in the harmonization of energy to awaken kundalini energy. Thus, you can look at the personality traits and characteristics as keys that can help unlock the lower mind. This wisdom can allow you to access supreme consciousness and not be limited by your natural weaknesses but instead harness your natural strengths. This is how astrology gives you the power to transmute your energy by working on yourself.

The twelve zodiac signs are not arbitrary but were formed by the ancients through observations that helped create mythology. The collective psyche on the planet, which is where mythology is derived, has made it so that mythologies of separate cultures share commonalities. Were the ancient philosophers and artists picking up on astrological frequencies when they wrote of legendary battles and personalities that shaped the very fabric of our nature? Know the signs and you will know people and yourself on an energetic level. You will also know what the planetary movements mean day by day because you will understand the energy. In a more practical sense, you'll know what to expect people to behave like as the planets move through signs, as well as how you will be feeling, so you will know what to do on each day to have a handle on your emotions.

ARIES: Ruled by Mars, this fire sign is confident, fast thinking, charismatic, and blunt.

TAURUS: Ruled by Venus, this earth sign is steady, loyal, stubborn, and enjoys the pleasures of the senses.

GEMINI: Ruled by Mercury, this air sign is curious, playful, talkative, and looks at both sides.

CANCER: Ruled by the Moon, this water sign is sensitive, loving, intuitive, and generous.

LEO: Ruled by the Sun, this fire sign is confident, outgoing, motivating, and fun.

VIRGO: Ruled by Mercury, this earth sign is detail oriented, thorough, organized, and nurturing.

LIBRA: Ruled by Venus, this air sign is eclectic, big hearted, friendly, and intellectual.

SCORPIO: Ruled by Pluto, this water sign is mysterious, sensual, investigative, and intense.

SAGITTARIUS: Ruled by Jupiter, this fire sign is adventurous, nature loving, and philosophical.

CAPRICORN: Ruled by Saturn, this earth sign is pragmatic, hardworking, and stable.

AQUARIUS: Ruled by Uranus, this air sign is big picture oriented, creative, intelligent, and independent.

PISCES: Ruled by Neptune, this water sign is artistic, loving, independent, and intuitive.

Houses

You can think of the houses like a giant clock. Each of the twelve houses relates to a part of our lives. By expanding our consciousness to this cycle, we are able to determine when it is best to do certain things in life, why we are experiencing certain things, and what we can expect. Like kundalini yoga, it is an analytical process that helps us understand our own energy. The houses also help reveal our soul blueprint, which is at the time of our birth. The in-depth study of the houses is beyond the scope of this book, but here is the area they each influence. The sign you have in each house at your time of birth greatly changes your core personality, preferences, and consciousness.

FIRST HOUSE: Represents our identity and self.

SECOND HOUSE: Governs our natural skills and talents we can make money with.

THIRD HOUSE: Our mind, siblings, and communication are governed by this house.

FOURTH HOUSE: This covers our home, family, and emotions.

FIFTH HOUSE: This house influences our creativity, intimacy, and manifesting ability.

SIXTH HOUSE: This represents our habits, health, and organization.

SEVENTH HOUSE: This has to do with our relationships, both business and marriage.

EIGHTH HOUSE: This is all about inheritances, shared finances, and sex.

NINTH HOUSE: This house is about learning and travel.

TENTH HOUSE: Career and public recognition are covered in this house.

ELEVENTH HOUSE: This is about friendships and our goals/dreams.

TWELFTH HOUSE: Our soul's growth opportunity is revealed in this house.

Rising Sign Horoscopes

When looking to utilize astrology to help harmonize your mind, body, and soul, reading horoscopes is sometimes where people start. What many people don't realize is that horoscopes are written in a way where it actually pertains more to your rising sign than your sun sign. That is a complicated thing to explain, but it is noted in order to help you get the most accurate and most helpful information from master astrologers. Your rising sign, also known as the ascendant, is easy to find in your birth chart, which is offered many places for free online. You will need your date of birth and the location and time of birth.

Transits

One of the best ways to use astrology to predict and understand emotional and psychological energy is to follow transits. It also will help you understand the birth chart and how specific positions of the planets are interpreted for you specifically. Each of the planets move through a sign for a different amount of time. It takes the Sun about a month to move through one of the twelve zodiac signs, while it takes the Moon just two and a half days. The planets that are farther away from the Sun take longer to go through a zodiac sign. The inner planets, which are closest to the Sun, include Mercury, Venus, Earth, and Mars. It takes Mercury fourteen to thirty days to move through one sign, it takes Venus about twenty-three to sixty days to move through a sign, and it takes Mars about one and a half months.

The outer planets, which include Jupiter, Saturn, Uranus, Neptune, and Pluto, take much longer. Jupiter stays in a sign for about a year, which means it takes twelve years to move through all the signs. Saturn stays in a sign for about three years, meaning it takes about twenty-eight to thirty years to move through all the signs. Uranus takes seven years in each sign, for an eighty-four-year full cycle through all twelve. Neptune spends a whopping fourteen years in a sign, which makes its full cycle 164 years. Pluto stays in a sign between fourteen and thirty years.

They say the outer planets like Pluto and Neptune are generational planets in that the theme of the sign they are in shapes the consciousness of an entire generation. You can see this as you trace the planet Neptune, which is about dreams and spirituality. When it was in Scorpio from 1957 to 1970, we saw the free love movement, which was people finding spiritual freedom through sexual exploration. As it moved through philosophical Sagittarius from 1970 to 1984, we saw a rise in social value of colleges and emphasis on academia. Then when it moved into Capricorn from 1984 to 1998, we saw the rise of financial corporations, which became the spiritual calling of the American dream. From 1998 to 2011 it moved through Aquarius and spurred the technology age. From 2012 to 2025 it moves through Pisces and is awakening our soul connection, our affinity for meditation as a culture, and our acknowledgement of intuition.

Tracking the planets as they change signs can greatly enhance your understanding of group consciousness, your own emotions, and the things that seem to happen randomly around you that are actually in response to greater energies at play. Having a basic understanding of the planetary energies which govern certain parts of our collective psyche is essential in understanding transits. In astrology, information builds upon itself. Similarly, knowing the personality and characteristics of each zodiac sign helps you understand how to harness the power of the universe.

Many people think that once they reach enlightenment, it will just be something to observe. However, the experience of seeing through the veil gives you the ability to cocreate with the universe. You can ride the tides, focus your energy, and create with energy. The power of enlightenment is very real and can help you get what you need in order to live a meaningful life. Understanding how to maximize our creative energy requires taking care of our physical body and keeping ourselves abreast of the energy that affects our physical body. When we aren't fighting against the currents of the cosmos but working with them, it's easier to stay in a high-vibrational state and manifest positive experiences.

Yugas

One of the most hopeful aspects of the long-standing system of astrology passed down by the yogis is the reliable cycle of the yugas. This large 25,000-year cycle tracks the rise and fall of civilizations. It follows the evolution and devolution of consciousness and helps explain the enlightened societies that existed in history as well as the more barbaric ones. The large cycle is divided into two halves of 12,500 years. During one half, society devolves in consciousness and then it evolves. We are currently at the turning point where we are becoming more evolved and will continue to do so for many thousands of years. The whole cycle is broken up into two thousand–year periods that correspond to the zodiac signs. We went through the two thousand–year cycle of the Piscean era last, where the "martyr consciousness" dominated. It made it easy for people to relate to the idea of Jesus giving up his life to save humanity or God giving up his son. It is easy to understand why the Christian symbol is the fish, which is also the symbol of Pisces.

Now we are just at the beginning of the Age of Aquarius. This is a new two thousand–year cycle where technology will continue to advance, telepathy will continue to develop, and we will see more evolved cultures where there is more peace and equality. Some say the Age of Aquarius started in 2012 when the Mayan calendar ended, and the kundalini yoga community marks the day 11/11/11 as the official start. Some astrologers say it likely started on the August eclipse of 1999, which helped kick it off in the year 2000. One of the main purposes of kundalini yoga is to enhance the self-sensory system of the subtle energy fields so that one can handle this shift to the Age of Aquarius. The teachings are focused on preparing one's nervous system to be able to handle the large amount of information we are now processing on a daily basis as well as be able to handle the EMFs now in our homes and atmosphere.

An Inspiring Story

In order to elucidate the very real effects of astrology on our lives, I want to share some fun stories. I began manifesting with the moon cycles each month and would always look forward to the fun things that would arrive for me and others at the time of the full moon. I distinctly remember telling a family member that the job they were trying to get would show up on the full moon. I was sitting right next to him when he received an unexpected call from a friend offering him a job on the full moon.

One month I wanted to manifest some very specific things. I would write down what I was looking to manifest each morning and night and knew that the full moon would likely bring them. I put down white tunics, as I needed them for yoga teaching. I didn't tell anyone that I was manifesting this, but I just did the energetic work of feeling like I had them and put positive energy toward it each day. At the full moon, I got a call that a friend of a friend had dropped off a few bags of clothes for me at their house. When I went through the clothes, it was remarkable that much of the free clothing was both new and mostly white tunics.

Another time, while working for a metaphysical company I really believed in, I wanted to help their company reach more people so I was working on manifesting media opportunities. More and more media companies kept reaching out to us to showcase our healers, and I was busy doing media events. The company even asked me to slow down on manifesting opportunities because they were having trouble keeping up with them. I did slow down, and the opportunities did as well. I then thought it might be nice for us to get some international and some paid exposure—and sure enough, when I focused on that, at the full moon an international and a paid opportunity presented themselves.

I also put little things on my manifesting list to work on my visualization and connection to energy. I put a gold ring and a rose on my list. When my roommate moved out that month, she gifted me a bracelet which had a gold ring on it, and one of my coworkers brought me a bundle of geraniums, which is a rose plant that happens to be my favorite scent of rose. It just goes to show how the creative force of the universe can surprise us and how the planets affect the outcome's timing significantly.

I had so much success in this process that I began teaching a class on it in Los Angeles. On the new moon, we would get together in a group of anywhere from five to twenty people. We would meditate and genuinely ask for universal guidance on what was in the highest good to manifest. We would record the idea on a vision board and then diligently visualize the goal for the next two and a half weeks until the full moon. Many students would return on the full moon and report the amazing experiences they had manifesting with the moon cycles where the exact thing on their board actually manifested.

In 2020 I also noticed how the releasing theme of the full moon that also hits our group consciousness played out with the suspension of presidential campaign announcements. Marianne Williamson suspended her run for president on the January 10 full moon. Elizabeth Warren suspended her presidential campaign just days before the March 9 full moon, and Bernie Sanders ended his campaign on the April 8 full moon. Full moon energy is powerful, and I'll never forget working the day after a full moon in a fire sign. Because the full moon was in Aries, people got into fights with their partners and many had blowout fights that led to breaking up. I was working as a professional clairvoyant and the day after this full moon in Aries, I received tons of calls from clients, all with the same story: they had had a fight with their partner and were devastated over the breakup. Over the years that I have been writing professionally about astrology, the theme of release and heightened energy has always played out.

11

Dreams and the Subconscious

Many cultures rely on dreams. In ancient Egypt, dreams were believed to be a prophetic link between the gods, spirits, and the lower world of humans. Egyptians used dreams to decide where to build temples, help cure illness, and make leadership decisions. Intuition was considered to be heightened in the dream state so that one could accurately predict the future. In Native American cultures, dreams are considered a sacred spiritual place where one can unite to an expanded state of consciousness. In this state one uses their knowledge of ancestors, land, and animals to understand the messages that come from universal consciousness.

Hebrews, Catholics, and Christians have long considered the dream world as a space where one could connect to God. The story of Joseph, who was cast out of his family because he saw he would lead Egypt in a dream, shows the power of someone who later became a dream interpreter for one of the pharaohs. In the bible there are countless stories of angels visiting people in dreams, as well such as Jacob wrestling with an angel in his dream. Aristotle believed dreams were the soul living separately from the body at nighttime. Sigmund Freud believed dreams were the desires of the repressed subconscious mind. Carl Jung expanded on this theory and believed the dream symbols were there to help reveal healing opportunities in a creative way.

What Happens When We Sleep

Our body enters the brainwave state of theta when we are in deep meditation, and this is also the state we are in when we are in a light sleep. In a deeper sleep, we enter into delta brainwaves, which are electrical brainwaves. When we are consciously dreaming in a state where we can direct our dream, we are able to explore and control our dream, but this is not a common state that most people experience. Some people do not remember their dreams, but the cleaner their diet is, the more likely they are to remember them. Clairvoyants use dreams to help heal their own energy field or clear it to become *clair* (clear) to be able to read their client's energy. They are essentially interpreting their own dreams to heal the energy of their own subconscious. But for some people, dreams can be extremely long, detailed, and traumatic, leaving one in a state of anxiety throughout the night and upon waking.

With the extensive value placed on dreams and interpreting them throughout both cultures and history, we see there is a link between them and the state of enlightenment, but how does it relate to kundalini energy? In order to understand this question, we need to understand how kundalini yogis are able to perceive and deal with the psychic pressure of the subconscious mind. They do this in order to raise their frequency and move past the subconscious instead of mucking about in it. The subconscious is essentially the garbage can of the mind. We can spend years trying to unlock our secret desires, heal our past wounds, or interpret obscure messages that may be symbolic or just projections of many memories jumbling together.

Dreams and Enlightenment

One huge part of the universal quest for enlightenment is our dreams and how they are interpreted in a spiritual manner. The modern human may see some level of entertainment in looking up what their strange dream means, but most do not take it too seriously because they haven't been able to understand the true nature of dreams and what is happening on an energetic level in the dream state. The reason that many cultures use dreams as a part of the spiritual healing process and as a big factor in the entire system of attaining enlightenment is because dreams are a direct reflection of the subconscious.

If you're not sure that dreams are a big part of the process of enlightenment, look at all the cultures who have looked to dreams to better interpret the true nature of the soul and existence. But to truly, really understand why dreams have been such a topic among divergent spiritual paths, we must understand the technical nature of the subconscious as well. Yogis have been studying the subconscious and its role in our own ability to reach enlightenment. As we look at the common themes in the way that we approach dreaming, we can begin to see just how big a role the subconscious plays as an opportunity to open the mystical door to nirvana, which is a transcendent state where you do not desire, suffer, or consider yourself as an individual.

We spend a significant amount of our time dreaming, but what most people don't see is that this dream state is directly linked to our perception of reality in waking consciousness as well as our ability to maneuver in it. It is perhaps the most misunderstood and overlooked connection in many systems that work on getting toward a state of enlightenment.

As with most concepts in kundalini yoga, it is best understood by experiencing it, and if you truly want to grasp the depth of this chapter, doing the kundalini yoga practices will be the best teacher. Dreams are used in modern times as a form of therapy, but perhaps even this therapy is only a temporary glimpse into the much bigger influential block to our experience of the ultimate state of peace. While some people perhaps are able to reach an expanded state of consciousness in a dream state, not everyone has the time to develop their intuition to that extent.

The majority of people are bombarded by their subconscious in their dreams; their bodies are taxed by recurring stress dreams, which makes it that much harder to handle the stress of waking life. The actual effects of stress dreams are significantly depleting, energetically speaking, and that is why the yogis found it useful to clear the subconscious and stop nightmares, which is quite a feat of consciousness mapping and navigation.

The Psychic Pressure of the Subconscious

Kundalini yogis have a sophisticated approach to understanding, talking about, and dealing with the subconscious mind that is a key part of their lifestyle and daily practice. All of this focus on understanding and overcoming the pressure of the subconscious mind is a very articulate way to see and move energy that blocks the raising of the kundalini, and this awareness and action ultimately helps activate it. Before we talk about how to clear the subconscious, we must really grapple with just how much the subconscious controls our life and blocks our ability to reach an enlightened state.

If you think of the subconscious as a living energy, each thought pattern or habit you have is alive in the subconscious. We know that like energy attracts like energy so whatever our subconscious is full of, those thoughts (electromagnetic wavelengths) will want more of them. Our mind will continue to search for similar thoughts, experiences, and feelings that will feed the energies of the subconscious to keep them thriving and growing. This is how neurosis develops and why people find themselves unable to break habits and not sure why they do things compulsively. The cyclical nature of our thoughts is hosting frequencies that also attract other like frequencies in the environment. When someone feels like their home is haunted, the fear of that haunting intensifies, bringing up more fears in their mind and attracting stronger spirits. The subconscious works without judgment of positive or negative; it just operates by the law of the universe that like attracts like. It directs the mind to think of things, speak things, be attracted to things, and pursue certain goals that will feed these thoughtforms. It really makes us out of control of our minds, words, actions, and goals. It is greatly influenced by the strong energy of group consciousness that is full of fear, addiction, anger, and the like.

The pressure that you can feel from the psyche or the subconscious is what makes you feel depressed, anxious, and lonely. It keeps you from perceiving possibilities, being creative, and breaking addictive behaviors. It can make it feel like you must have a drink to relieve the pressure or that you must yell to get something off of your chest. The addiction we get to anger, adrenaline, and self-pity is essentially very large and very hungry thoughtforms in the subconscious that exist in our energy field. This is why you can get a read on someone when you meet them. Your energy field is coming into contact with their energy field, so you get a download of the thoughtforms that essentially are running their mind. When you meet someone with a clear subconscious who has been scrubbing it for a long time each day, you're magnetized to them because their energy pulls you up temporarily. The large energy field of a healer is like a burst of pure life energy when you're around them, and it also agitates the lower vibrations of our traumatic memories, pushing them out or putting pressure on them to be faced and dealt with. Sometimes being in the presence of someone with really positive energy can make you cry because you feel how peaceful it could be if you weren't under the pressure of years of habitually negative and uncontrolled conditioning that has been deeply ingrained into your neural patterning.

This is not something you cannot control. In other words, you can control it, but you cannot just think your way out of it. Well, perhaps you can, but the chances of doing it successfully without falling into more fear-based thoughts is slim, and it would take a very long time. The lifestyle of kundalini yoga is primarily designed to keep your subconscious at bay, keep it cleared, and keep you elevated.

While we sleep, the subconscious is feeding on our energy by getting us to conjure images of our fears. Our guard is down in our mind and we cannot stop it from giving those psycho-magnetic thoughtforms more of the vibrations that keep them alive unless we use a stronger vibration day and night. For those who understand it, the battle of good and evil essentially is a vibrationally intelligent warfare.

Clearing the Subconscious to Expedite Enlightenment

Getting to a place where our vibration is high frequency requires clearing negative vibrations from the subconscious on a daily basis. While affirmations help, the trendy modern culture of thinking positively isn't enough to beat the generations of deeply ingrained fear-based thinking that doesn't allow us to direct the mind from a state of higher consciousness. Instead, most of us live and die, never realizing that we were just subject to the whims of the subconscious and barely glimpsing this feeling of enlightenment.

In order to get on with the healing and go past it, kundalini yogis developed a lifestyle that combats and clears the subconscious throughout the day. When you go to a kundalini class, you may not be used to someone talking at you about how to live the rest of the day; you may even feel affronted by it, but their wisdom is all about how to keep those heavy psycho-magnetic thoughtforms from creeping back into your life after class or between classes. The teacher knows that if the thoughtforms become too heavy, you're likely to fall back into your old patterns and stop coming to class.

So, when you hear them talking about walking around with a mantra in your head or playing mantras in your home, car, and office or while you sleep, they aren't just talking to hear their own voice. They know that their job is to lead you to a place of peacefulness and that most people have no tools to navigate their subconscious and mind. The yogis know the mind well and map the different states you go through on the path to overcoming the subconscious and then being able to direct the mind. Each part of their lifestyle is directed at this endeavor. The gong is certainly one of the most powerful, if not *the* most powerful, part of this daily practice, and mantras, breathwork, and glandular reset through yoga sets are all a part of it. The diet, the meditation, and the locks, which all work to keep your digestion, circulation, immune system, nervous system, organs, and brain functioning, will help you develop neural pathways that promote positive thinking habits and help you instead of hinder you in this quest for enlightenment. Does it happen instantly? No, but it does happen quickly. If you're doing one class a week and partying your ass off, it will be hard to notice a difference. The idea that kundalini yogis live the yogic lifestyle is not to show off or try to appear better than people; it is because it keeps them empowered, vibing high, and feeling good, period.

The reason playing mantras that are recorded in your own voice at night and doing the daily practice will help you is because your dream state will stop hindering your progress toward enlightenment. The wavelength of the mantra will stop the mind when your guard is down while sleeping. If you try sleeping with a mantra that is recorded with someone who doesn't have a strong navel connection, you may find it less effective than someone who does. A navel connection means that their voice is coming from their lower register, vibrating from the lower cavities of the body with the navel being pulled in a rhythm. This creates a specific frequency that helps stop nightmares. If you think of it as someone lying that speaks in a high pitch versus someone being brutally open and honest and their voice lowers, this can help you sense the frequency I speak of. You can also listen to mantras that are more operatic and stimulate the top of the head to stimulate the crown chakra. Recordings that are more baritone, with clear enunciation of plosives and vowels, will have a stronger effect. It may be hard at first to comprehend why, but once you have a strong daily practice reciting mantras using a rhythmic navel pump, you will get in tune with the heartbeat of the universe.

An Inspiring Story

In my personal experience, I have had different types of dreams: prophetic, notification of events as they happen, visitation from the deceased, and subconscious. One night I dreamed my best friend from college was pregnant. I texted her when I woke up to ask her if she was, and she said no. About two months later, she texted me saying that I was a witch because I knew she was pregnant before she did.

I also had a very interesting set of experiences with co-dreaming, where you are essentially in some realm of shared dream space. While living with my mother, we would sometimes wake up and have dreamed of the exact same thing that had the same details. We once dreamed of someone named Gil in the same night. In each of our dreams, the person was someone different, but both of us had the same name in our head. Another night we both dreamed of a camp, and then another night we both dreamed I was young and my parents were looking to buy land. I assumed this was because we were dreaming in the same room, but then I had another experience where my sister and I had a dream that revealed something that I didn't know had happened.

I was not living near my sister and didn't know what she was doing at the time. I had a vivid dream that her husband was sitting in a chair and she was telling him to get up, but he pointed to his feet, which were red and injured. I texted her in the morning because it seemed like a funny dream, and she said that she had dreamed he had tattooed socks on that same night. What was even more odd besides us both dreaming about his feet was that he said he had accidentally walked through a screen door and his feet were all scraped up. These experiences confirmed for me that there is a shared dream space or realm where we can access other consciousness.

I also have had vivid dreams for many years that often disturbed me so much I didn't want to go back to sleep and would wake up in a full sweat with a racing heartbeat. These stress dreams completely stopped when I started doing kundalini yoga, and for the first time in my life, I stopped dreaming altogether. I would lie down and not remember anything until I opened my eyes the next day. I also experimented with using night mantras for nightmares and found that my dreams didn't stop when I played them, but I didn't have nightmares when I played them. I also found that the lower-register mantras were more effective.

I have also had visitations from both living and deceased spiritual teachers in my dreams. One night I dreamed very vividly of a hawk as well as a man singing about how death should be celebrated as the next stage. I woke up and saw a text from my best friend that his grandfather had just passed, and I found out that hawks can represent the spirit passing. I have encountered other realms where I was aware I was in another realm and even encountered aliens and interacted with them in the dreamspace. When adding kundalini yoga practices, dreaming becomes an exciting mystical experience instead of energetic Russian roulette.

Yogi Bhajan

12

Our Common Search for Identity

It's clear by seeing our common discoveries as humans, despite cultural and chronological differences, that we desire to understand who we are. This seeking is something that yogis help us understand, and we can see that their mechanism of understanding the identity of human consciousness, the soul, and our joined experiences is desirable in that it helps us face life and death with a relaxed state of mind. It also motivates us to live life fully engaged in doing our best to help the common good. The fear of death is something that drives us to understand who we really are because without that understanding, things feel very finite, and ceasing to exist brings a sense of grief, as does the idea of separation from those we love.

The good news in our common endeavor for explaining our existence and identity is that there are so many experiences of spirits on the other side throughout cultures and throughout history. The way that yogis live their life to help people experience enlightenment and stop being afraid of death is not something most modern humans understand. They don't understand sitting and meditating or chanting for hours. They don't understand living without attachment or living with the passion to talk about such deep subjects as the soul and the subconscious. The modern human doesn't see why getting up before the body naturally wakes up is necessary or important. The entire priority system of yogis is to help ease suffering on the planet for all of us. This suffering comes from a lack of experience of the true identity and the fear of death. When we can experience who we truly are while alive, it helps us see death as just the next part of the soul's endless journey through multiple dimensions. The majority of modern humans live through the ego not because they reject enlightenment but because they don't have the keys or tools to access it and therefore are wholly unaware it exists or that it has such gifts to offer their emotional status.

The Cross-Cultural Experience of the Soul and Spirits

ANCIENT GREECE: Experiencing the spirit of a deceased person was normal in ancient Greece. It was considered good to have a spirit visit you in a dream if they were in a good state; if they appeared visibly, it was likely due to an unresolved issue. The need to offer proper burial and funeral rights is also seen in this culture to assist the soul in its journey.

AZTEC: Aztecs also believed the spirits of the deceased come visit the living, but the spirit's main goal was to be guided toward the next phase in their pursuit of reaching the ultimate state of happiness. They were buried with dogs and had dogs who were believed to be sacred protectors and guides, able to protect the living from unwanted spirits. The present holiday of el Día de los Muertos is from an ancient ritual honoring the spirits of the dead.

CELTIC: The spirits of the dead were believed to be around the living, and a day when it was easier to contact them was Samhain, which our modern Halloween stems from. Just as in other cultures, measures were taken to ward off angry spirits as you wouldn't invite an angry neighbor into your house.

CHINA: Honoring the ancestors to obtain blessings was common. There are holidays to honor the deceased, and it is also common for the spirit to visit either in a dream or a vision. The ancestors are essentially worshipped and revered because there is strong recognition of the power that spirits have over the living and how they can greatly influence someone's life.

EGYPTIAN: The afterlife, preparation for it, and protection of it was a major part of Egyptian life. If a person lived a good life, they would go on to a happy afterlife. It was common for spirits to return and resolve wrongs that were done to them by visiting the living even if they only found out after death. Tombs were not to be disturbed because it was believed this would disturb the spirit, just as many other cultures believe. Additionally, Egypt and many other cultures honor the dead to receive blessings from the spirits by protecting their graves.

INDIA: In India there is a belief in the afterlife of the soul and that spirits of the deceased come back to bother the living if there is a problem or just peacefully as well (often in dreams). The cremation ritual is to ensure the spirit doesn't try to re-enliven the body. They believe if someone lived a virtuous life, their spirit continues into the rebirth phase as an evolved soul. However, if they were non-virtuous, their spirit can get demoted to a harder life when they are reborn, offering them the opportunity for spiritual growth. Spirits are also known to stick around sometimes for one reason or another and visit people.

MESOPOTAMIA: It was believed that spirits enter another state after death and that these two realms were intended to remain separate. There were many rituals to make sure a spirit had what it needed in the afterlife as if it needed energetic nourishment. It was known that problems in one's lives were often because their ancestors were unhappy with them or other spiritual beings were trying to show them how to do better, teaching them from the other side. Essentially spirits would appear to the living for very important reasons.

Finding Peace Beyond the Ego

The reason for bringing up all of these ancient cultures that all recognized the role spirits have in life is to highlight the present-day schism with this belief and practice. Many people scoff at the idea of an afterlife but perhaps are unaware of how prevalent the experience of actually seeing a spirit is worldwide. Presently, most of modern Western civilization has no firm grasp of the concept that death is only a transition as the ancients did. If presented with the irrefutable evidence of the existence of spirits, this would likely change. Today many mediums can prove that spirits exist by bringing up facts about their lives and the people they knew. While mediumship pops up in mainstream society, there is still a stigma surrounding it. Shadows have been cast on intuitive abilities as inauthentic and immature in a society founded on patriarchal systems valuing reason over emotional intelligence.

The ego, which identifies as finite and separate from the energy of life, creates goals that are self-serving because that is the nature of the ego: preservation. But when the mind doesn't perceive or experience the higher state of consciousness, the ego, obsessed with preservation, becomes inverted in a way that doesn't allow for the experience of connection to more than the individual temporary personality and physicality. This shortness of sight, for lack of a better term, is a terrible lack of wisdom and happiness for most people because culturally they are shunned from seeking something that can provide a real sense of peace. Instead they are condemned to go through life not talking about death, not wondering if there is something more, and joking about their feelings. The ego is not designed to be the guide of our mind because it cannot use wisdom to decide but rather uses its environment to deduce. It does not have the bigger picture, and it does not allow us to make choices that bring us sustained, deep satisfaction, although it will push us to seek satisfaction.

Facing Death and Overcoming Fear of Dying

It's entirely possible and commendable to live a modern life and a yogic lifestyle instead of thinking black-and-white about it. You can own a business, have a family, and still grapple with the deeper aspects of the identity of the human as a soul. You can and very much should engage in society, make money, study subjects, and become successful, but incorporating a yogic lifestyle will allow you to do it all without depression, addiction, and fear. The truth is, a yogic lifestyle can make you very successful. When you understand the true nature of energy, thoughts, and the mind, you will be able to overcome your own blocks to health, happiness, and success, but you won't need external validation to feel content. You will be okay if you lose a limb, a job, a friend, a partner, or even your sight. The experience of the awakening of kundalini allows you to see the bigger picture of who you are so that what happens in your life doesn't control your happiness. If you simply work each day to cultivate that awareness by doing things that raise your kundalini energy, you can walk and live peacefully, knowing you are living now and will continue to live in different forms.

If we are going to overcome our addictions, depressions, and self-destructive behaviors, we will need to change our daily habits in order to have the energy to tap into universal consciousness. If we continue to deny the existence of the continuity of the soul, thinking that somehow science doesn't support it, we will only deny ourselves greater levels of happiness and block our culture from experiencing greater levels of joy. There is one undeniable truth among all of this, which is that people desire to be happy and they desire others to be happy. If we approach the idea of kundalini as a universal experience of enlightenment, knowing that each person is flawed and each system is not a perfect system, we can see the common themes that wish to distill our true identity and accept that there is a universal consciousness and spiritual realm we can tap into.

The point of this book, if you have arrived at the final chapter, is merely to help you see some simple ways to access greater levels of happiness for yourself and your loved ones. It is not to promote Sikhism, one person's personal fame or agenda, or any religion; it is merely to show common themes across history that hint at our common desire, experience, and potential. If you want to begin, just adopt small changes. Maybe start with the tea and a few minutes of breathwork or doing an online class. Maybe look at incorporating more fruits and vegetables. Don't think you need to be extreme to reach enlightenment, and you'll end up where you need to be.

An Inspiring Story

Growing up, I was very afraid of death. I clung to people, their opinions, and my own life. I was afraid of dying and of losing pets, friends, and family members. I felt as if life was a pretty scary place, with death looming over me. When I started taking the clairvoyant training program, I started to understand the spirit world and connect with it in meditation. I had a few instances where spirits told me information I hadn't known before that I was later able to verify. It was a really inspiring experience to know that there was another realm beyond the physical world. I stopped feeling so pressured to control my life and fit in when I realized that I was just a soul here many times trying to help the world. I realized that I didn't need to let the opinions of others dictate my life. I found meditation to be an exciting space where I didn't know what I would find.

Once Yogi Bhajan told me a date and the word "orange." He is deceased and this seemed quite strange. I looked up the date and it was a day off, but there was a whole long story he had told in a lecture on that day about oranges and how his spiritual teacher had told him to take them from an orchard and give them to the poor. In my clairvoyant training, I witnessed other people contacting the deceased, and they were able to bring through exact information for other people in the room.

Now I feel more at peace on a daily basis. I don't feel the need to make a certain amount of money to feel good enough, nor do I feel the need to adhere to society's beauty standards to feel self-worth. I meet people who live a humble lifestyle and have been influenced by a culture that has a spiritual core, and they are much happier, nicer, and more peaceful than the modern technology-addicted, ego-driven American. We are obsessed with things that don't bring us happiness. From living all over the United States, taking Buddhist meditation and yoga classes, working and living with people from all over the world with different backgrounds and constantly breaking my own self-imposed limits of what I think life needs to look like, I've found that life isn't going to be perfect, but we can still feel connected, peaceful, and happy even when it's not.

I began writing books while undergoing chronic pain. It pushed my nerves, emotions, and mind to the limit. I was barely able to get through the day, and things like walking my dog or doing the dishes were extremely painful.

This went on for two years, and what got me through it was holding on to my true soul identity, knowing that as long as I am focused on helping people, that is enough. I went to bed knowing that even if I was struggling, I felt good about who I was, what I was living for, and that being kind was always an option even with physical barriers that made life difficult.

To me, practicing and teaching kundalini yoga has felt nothing short of miraculous and magical. I've experienced a state of happiness that I never had previously and can say that there's something to it. It really does work, and it really does have tremendous implications for helping humanity even more than it already has.

Conclusion

*R*eading this book will not give you the experience of enlightenment. Sitting and listening to a guru will not either. Only you can give that to yourself, and this knowledge is quite possibly the most empowering bit of information you will ever receive. You must fine-tune your trifecta of mind, body, and spirit to harness your own energy and activate your potential to be a self-realized soul/human. You are now equipped with things you can do each day to achieve the experience of enlightenment and beat your negative mind. These days it seems the world is rampant with fear; that's nothing new, but with the study of astrology we have seen that there are predictable cycles of history, and for our lifetime, we are on the upswing to evolved, more enlightened civilization. We will continue to see the trends of astrology, meditation, spiritual classes, and healthy living spread around the world as we evolve. We can all get on board the speedway to enlightenment with the accessible and universal practices in kundalini yoga while still participating in the belief systems that we feel most comfortable with. You do not have to change your beliefs to change your diet. You do not have to change your political party affiliations to add some breathing exercises into your day. You do not even have to completely grasp what the experience of enlightenment offers you in order to start doing some of the things in this book.

No one really can grasp enlightenment until they experience it. Perhaps you've experienced enlightenment in other lifetimes and it is a latent memory begging to be revisited. Even if you have not and you feel that somehow you are not worthy of something that has been written about with such reverence, you are. For all the lowly moments of our lives, we can live just as pure and loving. It doesn't matter where we have been, how we have lived our lives, or what we have done; we can always shift our energy and alchemize our reality. While the old beliefs we started our journey with will still exist, we may simply expand to see more of what once was out of scope because the view was simply a small picture of a much larger reality. If you were to take a telescope and look at another planet and all you saw was one thing, you might assume that all foreign life was like that one thing and miss the many more evolved parts of that planet with different levels of consciousness. If someone were to look at our planet and see a slug and think that was all that was here, they would also miss a lot of the life and reality that they were unable to perceive. May this book continue to help you widen your viewpoint to experience the vast beauty and amazing truths of human existence. May it inspire you to accept and love all people, regardless of differences, and may it help you find and accept yourself.

This book empowers you to know that while there is not just one way to reach enlightenment, surely so many cultures with common practices over so many time periods and in so many parts of the world are onto something. It's reassuring and hopeful for the future of humanity and the peace of all people that we come to understand this. If we realize that it's not about proving our way is right but about seeing we are all trying to reach and explain the same phenomena, perhaps we will be one step closer to finding peace with each other. When we implement a practice that resonates with us, we can also be tremendously hopeful that our minds can be free of fear, anger, and hatred, and find a true sense of lasting happiness regardless of our external life circumstances.

References

3HO. "Mudra." 2021. https://www.3ho.org/kundalini-yoga/mudra.

———. "Pranayam Techniques." 2021. https://www.3ho.org/kundalini -yoga/pranayam/pranayam-techniques.

Abramson, Ashley. "Substance Use During the Pandemic." American Psychological Association. March 1, 2021. https://www.apa.org /monitor/2021/03/substance-use-pandemic.

Adams, Tom. "Kundalini and Tibetan Buddhism." 2001. https:// easternhealingarts.com/kundalini-and-tibetan-buddhism.

Aizenstate, Steve. "Here's What These Ancient Cultures Believed About Dreams." *Dream Tending*. February 22, 2019. https://dreamtending .com/blog/what-do-dreams-mean-ancient-cultures/.

Bhajan, Yogi. *The Aquarian Teacher*. 2005. Kundalina Research Institute.

Brown, Cathy. "15 Sacred Plants from Cultures Around the World." July 28, 2014. https://matadornetwork.com/bnt/15-sacred-plants -around-world/.

Cassaro, Richard. "Discovery of the Third Eye in the Ancient Americas." November 18, 2015. https://www.richardcassaro.com/tag/third-eye -aztecs-kundalini-yoga-maya/.

Cultural Awareness International. "Fasting Around the World." January 22, 2015. https://culturalawareness.com/fasting-around-the-world/.

Foreman, Chad. "The Four Main Spiritual Practices of Tibetan Buddhism." *Uplift*. November 28, 2016. https://upliftconnect.com /four-main-spiritual-practices-tibetan-buddhism/.

Hays, Jeffrey. "Brahmins." *Facts and Details*. 2008. http://factsanddetails .com/india/Religion_Caste_Folk_Beliefs_Death/sub7_2b/entry -4181.html.

———. "Mongol Religion in the Times of Genghis Khan." *Facts and Details*. April 2016. http://factsanddetails.com/central-asia /Mongolia/sub8_2b/entry-4575.html.

Institute for Consciousness Research. "Kundalini in Egypt." n.d. https:// www.icrcanada.org/learn/historicalbasis/kundalini-egypt.

———. "Kundalini in India." n.d. https://www.icrcanada.org/learn /historicalbasis/kundaliniindia.

Koithan, Mary, and Cynthia Farrell. "Indigenous Native American Healing Traditions." *The Journal for Nurse Practitioners: JNP* 6, 6 (2010): 477–78. doi:10.1016/j.nurpra.2010.03.016.

Lipson, Elaine. "Unravelling the Mystery of Tibetan Yoga Practices." *Yoga Journal*. August 29, 2007. https://www.yogajournal.com /yoga%20-101/mystic/.

Mark, Joshua J. "Ghosts in the Ancient World." *World History Encyclopedia*. October 30, 2014. https://www.worldhistory.org /ghost/.

Millar, Jennifer. "What Is the Dantian and Why Is It Important?" 2019. http://www.jennifermillar.org/what-is-the-dantian-and-why-is-it -important.

Morgan, Karina. "Psychedelic Yoga: New Twist on Ancient Practice." *Third Wave.* June 22, 2019. https://thethirdwave.co/psychedelic-yoga/.

Prakash, M., and J. Carlton Johnny. "Things You Don't Learn in Medical School: Caduceus." *Journal of Pharmacy & Bioallied Sciences* 7, Suppl 1 (2015): S49–S50. doi:10.4103/0975-7406.155794.

Research the Truth. "The Trinity Is a Pagan Concept." n.d. http://www .researchthetruth.com/christian/paganism4.html.

Setting Sun Wellness. "What Is Breathwork?" December 23, 2017. http:// www.settingsunwellness.com/blog/what-is-breathwork.

Sidorova, Anna. "Planets and Subtle Body: How Planet Energies Are Related to Chakras." *Exemplore.* June 25, 2020. https://exemplore .com/astrology/Planets-And-Subtle-Body-How-Planet-Energies-Are -Related-To-Chakras.

Temperance, Elani. "Fasting." *Witches and Pagans.* September 29, 2012. https://witchesandpagans.com/pagan-paths-blogs/fasting.html.

United Nations. "World Drug Report 2019: 35 Million People Worldwide Suffer from Drug Use Disorders While Only 1 in 7 Receive Treatment." June 26, 2019. https://www.unodc.org/unodc/en/frontpage/2019 /June/world-drug-report-2019_-35-million-people-worldwide-suffer -from-drug-use-disorders-while-only-1-in-7-people-receive-treatment .html.

Weaver, Sandra. "Quetzalcoatl Is Deeper Than Just a Mayan Story of Myth." *Spiritual Growth Prophecies.* 2008–2014. http://www.2012 -spiritual-growth-prophecies.com/quetzalcoatl.html.

Winn, Michael. "Taoist Yoga and the Kundalini." June 25, 2019. https:// www.energygatesqigong.us/healing-energy/taoist-yoga-and-the -kundalini.html.

YB Teachings. "Prana, Vayus, Nadis and Kundalini." *Yogi Bhajan Lecture Archive.* 2002. http://fateh.sikhnet.com/sikhnet/articles.

Index

To Write to the Author

If you wish to contact the author or would like more information about this book, please write to the author in care of Llewellyn Worldwide and we will forward your request. Both the author and the publisher appreciate hearing from you and learning of your enjoyment of this book and how it has helped you. Llewellyn Worldwide cannot guarantee that every letter written to the author can be answered, but all will be forwarded. Please write to:

Shannon Yrizarry
℅ Llewellyn Worldwide
2143 Wooddale Drive
Woodbury, MN 55125-2989

*Please enclose a self-addressed stamped envelope for reply
or $1.00 to cover costs. If outside the USA, enclose
an international postal reply coupon.*

Many of Llewellyn's authors have websites with additional information and resources. For more information, please visit our website:

WWW.LLEWELLYN.COM